# THE GENIUS
# IN CHILDREN

## Bringing out the best
## in your child

BY

RICK ACKERLY

Library of Congress Catalog Number: 2009933860
Printed in the United States of America
First Printing: 2010

Cover design by Jay Monroe
Interior design and layout by Kristen Hall

# THE GENIUS
# IN CHILDREN

Kenton —
It has been so
terrific getting to know
you and your wonderful
family. Please stay in
touch - email me often
w/ stories. It's my
life's blood.
Thank you for everything,
Rick
6-11-10

*To my grandchildren*
*Annlyn, Aasha, Elijah, and Abdallah*

# CONTENTS

Introduction: Into the Woods    1

## I: Play Position

1. Parents: The First Teachers    11
2. Discipline    16
3. Education    23
4. Character, Integrity, and Virtue    27
5. Air-Traffic Controller    32
6. Getting Our Children to Talk    37
7. Making Them Strong, Letting Them Go    40
8. Mr. Rick, Air-Traffic Controller    43

## II: Self Do It

9. Self Do It    51
10. Boundary-Setting    57
11. We Are All New    62
12. Getting Our Butterflies to Fly in Formation    66

## III: It's Academic

13. Engaging Genius    73
14. Freedom to Read    82
15. Acceleration    89
16. Abilities, Disabilities, and Success    97
17. Being Literate    106

## IV: Letting Them Struggle

*(Struggle, Failure, Disappointment, Loss, and Suffering Are Opportunities)*

18. Getting Our Geniuses to Dance Together     113
19. Holding Their Hand When They Suffer     117
20. Living in the Tension     121
21. What Comes Then Goes     125
22. Enthusiastic Struggle     128
23. Which Way Success?     132

## V: "Normal," Difference, and the Pursuit of Genius

24. Real Men Wear Pink     139
25. What's "Normal"?     143
26. Greatness     148
27. The Sound of Silence     150
28. Anatomy of a Miracle     154

## VI: Staying Out of Trouble

29. Don't Throw Me in That Briar Patch     163
30. Getting Your Comeuppance     169

## VII: Good, Bad, and Integrity

*(Make Friends with the Monster Under the Bed)*

31. Safe to Be Bad     185
32. Violence and Evil     189
33. The Discipline of Patience     194

# VIII: Let Them Teach You

*(Be Open to Learning about Yourself*
*as You Teach Your Children)*

34. What Would Be the Smart Thing?                    201
35. Making Mistakes                                   204
36. Who's Going to First Grade?                       206
37. Who's Saving Whom?                                209
38. Being True to Your Genius                         212


Epilogue: Mantras for Working with Children          218
Appendix                                             220
Acknowledgments                                      222
Notes                                                226

# Introduction:
# Into the Woods

**gen·ius** *n* 1. The tutelary spirit of a person, place, or institution.
  —*The New Oxford American Dictionary*, 2001

One day when my daughter Brooke was one, she decided to take a walk. She opened the screen door to our summerhouse, stepped onto the flagstone walk, and headed down the dirt road that led into the woods. She walked with a purpose. She didn't say anything. She didn't even look at me. In fact, it was as if I weren't there. She just stood up from the pots and pans she had been banging on the kitchen floor, made for the screen door, and pushed it open.

As you can imagine, my first reaction was to stop her. I thought, "I can't let a child that age, who has barely learned how to walk, just walk out the door without even checking with me. Where could she be going? All sorts of things could happen to her. A responsible father does not let his one-year-old daughter take off into the woods on her own. It's just too dangerous."

In that first second, another thought arose: "Wait—there is no immediate danger. Let's just keep an eye on her and see what happens. I don't have to act . . . yet." And so I just watched.

As these thoughts collided, I detected the barest flicker of yet another thought: "She is acting as if she knows what she is doing!" Now, when people act as if they know what they are doing, I hesitate to interfere with their decisions. And Brooke's whole demeanor communicated "I don't need your help." So I decided to follow her.

By the time she reached the dirt road that led into the woods, I had something of a plan. Somehow, I had to do four things at once: keep out of the situation, watch her, let her go, and keep her safe. A voice from deep inside told me that her decision to do this on her own needed to be honored. She did not look around for me, so I didn't call her attention to my presence, but instead followed at a careful distance, hiding behind trees and sneaking around corners, hoping she wouldn't see me. And she didn't.

As she trod the dusty gravel, shadows of leaves played on her hair. I kept my feet to the tire tracks, where I'd be less likely to kick a stone or break a stick. Around the first corner, she skirted the mud puddle. Taking the second corner, she looked up at the giant paper birch. She seemed almost to march as she followed the winding road all two hundred yards of its length through the woods.

When she came to the place where the driveway met the main road that went around the lake, she looked to the right and to the left just like an adult, or an older child who had been listening to adults about looking both ways. Her demeanor said, "This is my world, and I am comfortable in it." Fearless, she seemed to be mapping out her place in this world: "Let's see, what's down this way? What's up that way?" She paused for a couple of seconds, as if to ponder the situation, and then, very decisively, turned around and started home.

When she got back to the house, she went back to her place on the floor as if nothing special had happened and, still, as if I weren't even there. She did not come running to me so I could welcome her home. She did not tell me about her adventure. It was something she had done, and it was complete.

In the summer of 1967, in the outback of Connecticut—Litchfield County—I judged the environment safe enough for this adventure. There were wild animals, but the only ones I had seen in fifteen years were, as we said, "more afraid of us than we are of them." Cars were a danger, but they did not come down the driveway often, and they usually came slowly when they did.

Nonetheless, I am sure many parents would find my behavior at that moment in Brooke's life irresponsible. I am sure most parents would not have let her wander on her own. They might have stopped her. They might have gone with her. I am pretty sure they would not have done what I did. It is not normal parent behavior, these days, to let a child launch off into the world on her own like that—certainly not at that age. And yet, as I look back forty-some years later, for that child in that moment, it was an example of brilliant parenting. Would that I were always so brilliant.

What inspired Brooke's adventure? After all these years of fathering, teaching, and running schools, I think I know. At least, I have chosen a name for it: genius. The ancient Greeks called it *kharakter,* the Romans called it genius, a great science teacher I know called it "the teacher within," and we all have it. According to James Hillman[1] and Thomas Moore,[2] it goes by many names: soul, muse, calling, psyche, and destiny. It is the *you* that is becoming. It is our inner author and the source of our authority in the world.

More important than naming it, I have learned to trust it. In fact, I know trusting that "something" is the bedrock of all effective work with children—and, for that matter, with all people. As an educator, I have learned that believing in it, watching for it, encouraging it, and letting it work its way out into the world is the secret of education.

Our children are on their own journey. This journey is guided by their soul. In attempting to participate in their education, we have to partner up with their genius. This book is about the disciplines of such partnering.

**Our children are on a journey guided by their souls.**

Believing in your child and her genius is not so hard at first. Even though a child's flaws and shortcomings show up almost immediately, most parents are able to maintain their wonderment at the divine perfection of their children right up to the first day of school. But school often puts this belief at risk:

"Amy clung to my leg the whole time, and finally the teacher had to pull her off me. She was the only one. The other girls went straight to the climbing structure, all shouts and laughter."

"Pete doesn't tell me anything. I'm all, 'How was school today?' and he's like, 'Fine.'"

"The other kids in the car are reading road signs. Sara is clueless, she can't even read 'Cookies' off the cookie jar."

"Farida won't practice the piano. I am spending all this money on lessons, and she refuses to practice."

"Be thankful she plays music at all—Ali can't carry a tune."

"Cameron is always getting into fights."

"Jamie won't stand up for herself."

"—PLACE YOUR COMPLAINT HERE—"

Whoever your child, he or she will give you something to worry about before the end of fourth grade. Either that or you were not given the worry gene.

When our children go off to school, parenting acquires other layers of challenge. When they say goodbye to us at the school-house door for the first time, we know—we feel deeply—that we have been taken to the next level of parenting. We now have to watch, protect, help, love, and support from one step removed. We have to rise to all the challenges of parenting through and with others, from a distance, and with mostly secondhand information (if we get any at all). When the children go around the next corner, they vanish. They are out of sight. They are having their adventures under the watchful (one hopes) eye of someone else.

How can parents handle these new challenges effectively? How can we learn from them? What should we do when Isaac won't get up in the morning? When Mattie keeps getting into trouble? What about dyslexia and the dreaded ADHD? How do we help Ellen stand up to peer pressure?

What if our children are harassed? What if their report cards or their test scores are disappointing? What if the homework looks too easy? Too hard? What if they fail? What do you do when your child comes home and says, "Nobody will play with me!" or "The science teacher doesn't know how to teach!"?

What do you do if you hear from another parent that your child is being picked on by the teacher—and your child has said nothing about it? What if your son starts getting interested in boys—and vice versa?

What do you do when your son starts using language or behavior you know he never learned at home? When your children try to play you and your partner against each other? How do you get Marilyn to clean up her room or to do her home-work? How do you get Wayne to obey you?

Parents have been bringing me questions like this for many years, and of course, the list is nearly as diverse as the kinds of people in the world—that's why education has kept me interested for so long. Very few such questions have generic answers that are any good, because people are different and each relationship is unique. Hence, this is a book of moments in the lives of children, their parents, and their teachers. These are stories of unique characters in action. They do, however, illuminate some of the principles of education and some of the disciplines we need to be good stewards of our children's genius.

The stories are not presented as blueprints for success. You will probably never have an opportunity to copy them. This is not a list of rules that you won't remember anyway in moments of crisis. There is no formal training for parenthood as there is for teachers, and this book is not intended to fill this gap. The vignettes in this book are designed to provide both delight and enjoyment in the miracle of it all, and perspective and solace in the difficulty of it all. They put parents and teachers everywhere in the same communion: people who have decided to take responsibility for children and know that, to be effective, they have to keep finding the job inspiring.

Whether or not you worry about your children, whether or not you can hang on to that wonderment at their divine perfection, our number-one job as parents and educators is to notice the children in our care and to delight in them. I hope this book will help you both notice and delight, as well as give you perspective and guidance on how to overcome your fears and offer an idea or two about how to handle tough situations.

If I could be granted one wish for our children it would be that their parents and their teachers would keep their focus on the long run, entrusting the trials, struggles, and sufferings of the short run to the kids. I propose a shift in focus from test scores to enthusiasm, from getting into high school and college to getting the most out of it when you get there, from perfect behavior to learning from mistakes, from measuring up to making something of yourself, from independence to interdependence, from goodness to integrity, from fear to love.

All these stories are *true*. This is not to say that all the details are presented precisely as they happened. For one thing, some of the names have been changed, though some have not. Some stories are composites of several stories, and some of the people are composites of several people. If, on reading a story, you decide that you are one of the parents, teachers, or students in this book, I am glad that something has resonated enough for you to think so. Know, however, that not only the names but also some of the specifics have been changed. None of this is about you. It is all about us.

# I: Play Position

# 1.

# Parents: The First Teachers

Recently, the daughter of a friend sent me the following e-mail in response to my "From the Principal's Office" column on the website www.DivineCaroline.com:

*Dear Rick,*

*As a mom, I often feel that I am hanging on by my fingertips. I'll tell you why I don't read the how-to books on parenting: It's because I can't parent with one hand and have the recipe book in the other. I need both hands, and sometimes both feet. Actually, most of the time I need my whole body and my mind and my heart focused on my children. I am pouring everything that is me into all that they are. When I get into bed, I have gone to bed because I can't stay awake anymore, so I am not going to read myself to sleep with a good book telling me all the rules of parenting I violated today. I also don't need some guy (or woman either) telling me what to do.*

*As the mother of a seven-year-old and a two-year-old, my secret parenting self-medication when I am feeling confused and overwhelmed is discovering that there are others out there going through the exact same thing. That is why I am addicted to* The Nanny *and* Shalom in the Home. *I love hearing about the bad behaviors and how they are resolved. I am craving reminders about why I am doing this and that I am not alone.*

*That's why I like your articles. In this era of "helicopter" parenting and the expectations we place on our kids, hearing the principal's point of view is terrific. Since the parents are the original and the best teachers of our kids, how do we teach well? We know how to love 'em; how do we make 'em resilient and brave? Especially now that my oldest is off at school. It is different being the parent of a child away, and there isn't much on the subject.*

*Gail*

Yes, the parent is the child's first teacher. I would add that parents continue to be the child's primary teachers all the way through school. That is not to say, however, that parents should try to be *the* teacher.

While it is good for parents to see themselves as *educators*, it is critical that "parents" and "teachers" play their respective positions. The main reason why parents should not take on the role of teacher is because it is bad for children. You can see this quite clearly in a sound parental approach to reading.

As parents, parents *should* read to their children every evening before they go to bed. The main purpose is that it is good for the relationship; secondarily, it is the age-old way of passing the culture on to our children (the old storytelling thing); thirdly, it is good for language development; and lastly, it helps them in their natural process of learning how to read. Most parents I know do this quite naturally. My wife, Victoria, did that with her daughter Lizzie with very few exceptions. When Lizzie was in bed with teeth brushed and pj's on, Victoria would come in,

Lizzie would ask for a book, and off they would go into their own little world together—sometimes for a half-hour.

Even after Lizzie learned to read on her own, she would often want her mom to do the reading. By the age of seven years or so, this bedtime ritual had morphed into a mother-daughter talk—a ritual that is still going on today, ten years later.

One evening, as I was going down the stairs past the open door of Lizzie's room, I heard: "Mom, can this be one of those times when I can tell you anything and you won't get mad?"

"Yes," I heard her respond. "You can say anything, and I won't get mad, and I won't be hurt."

Of all the educational experiences Lizzie has had in her fourteen years of excellent education, I believe that this has been one of the most important.

But in our culture, the lives of schoolchildren are distorted by READING!!!!! Reading has become this do-or-die thing that must be done by age six and a half or "my child will be below average," and being below average is the kiss of death. Once you are below average, you stay below average for the rest of your educational career, and that will doom you to . . . or worse and . . . you can finish the paragraph.

None of this is true, of course, and in their right minds, most parents laugh at this kind of talk. However, when their child is slow to read, it is not uncommon for parents to lose their minds and go into a tailspin of fear-driven behavior that can have detrimental side effects for the child.

One of the negative side effects is that parents begin to turn home time into teaching time. All too often, parents take on the responsibility of teaching academic skills. When this happens, the child begins to feel surrounded by teachers. He can feel cornered and become increasingly anxious or angry, sometimes to the point of shutting down as a student, as if to say, "OK, I quit. This isn't any fun anymore. If you guys think you can pound this into me, go right ahead. I'll have nothing of it. I am going to go play. After all, that is my job. I am a kid, remember?"

Teaching the child to read is the job of the school and the teachers in it. It is not the job of the parent. Children need teachers at school and parents at home. They are happy to go to school; they want to learn; they want to learn all they can learn; they want to learn to read. By first grade, they are dying for homework. We can take that enthusiasm for learning away from them if **a)** we care more about it than they do, **b)** we get worried about their success, **c)** we make them give up play (which is a child's right) to take on schoolwork, and **d)** we turn their parents into teachers.

**Children need teachers at school and parents at home.**

Ryan's parents wanted Ryan to come to our school. Although he was still only five years old, they thought that it was important to make sure he was prepared academically. In their conversations with me, they wanted to make sure that I was impressed with how hard they had been working to get Ryan up to speed in the skills of writing and reading and arithmetic. They were particularly proud of a new technique they were using: flash cards in the bathtub. When Ryan visited in the classroom, however, he was the only one of twelve students who was unable to pursue his own interests, work with others, and engage in the activities. He kept looking at the teacher for direction. In their conscientious attempt to make sure that Ryan was prepared, his parents were inadvertently undermining his ability to do what kindergarten would require of him. Their focus on academics (the job of the teacher) was ruining him as a student.

We simply have to play position, letting the child play hers.

Playing position is mostly a matter of being clear about who is supposed to make what decisions, and being sure that we play the parent position well. We don't want to interfere with our teammates: our child, our parenting partner, our child's teacher, or other caregivers. Sometimes this means deciding not to act at all, perhaps just saying, "Oh?" or "Oh!" or just "Oh."

A moment of decision often requires a balance of two very sound educational principles, such as "Treat children as if they know what they are doing" and "Don't ask your children to make decisions they are not ready to make." We have to find the balance between keeping children safe and letting them learn from their mistakes, between letting them struggle and letting them go, between setting limits for them and letting them discover boundaries on their own, between protecting them and letting them get their comeuppances, between letting them fight their own battles and stepping in. These moments of decision are endless, and making the best one is not about which option is better; it is about who should decide, and when and how . . . and the hardest decisions come when you least expect them.

Playing position is a matter of seeing your child as an authority while continuing to exercise your own. How can both people be the authority? It's tricky, and finding the answer is the secret to a long and happy life in a world with other people. The central question is: Who gets to exercise his or her decision-making muscle, you or your child?

Play position. Always play position.

# 2.

# Discipline

∾

The concept of genius to which this book is dedicated is the classic, not the modern, meaning. In the last few generations genius has taken on the connotation of superiority. My son Peter has warned that it may be an act of *hubris* to try to resurrect its meaning of a power unique and incomparable that each of us has.

The word "discipline" has similarly lost much of its original meaning in the last fifty years. When I look "discipline" up in a thesaurus, nine of the twelve words have negative connotations. Here are the top two definitions on Microsoft Word 2004:

1. the practice or methods of ensuring that people obey rules by teaching them to do so and punishing them if they do not
2. a controlled orderly state, especially in a class of schoolchildren

These definitions are not useful; actually they are destructive of education. I must, therefore, try to get us back to using the original meaning. Discipline is a good thing—an unmitigated good thing. Discipline is actually the behaviors, habits, and attitudes that help us accomplish our goals. What could be bad about that? Discipline is what children need in order to make something of themselves. Discipline is what we need in order to be good stewards of our child's genius. Discipline is required to play position properly.

Many fifth-grade teachers give their students the homework for the week on Monday, rather than giving one assignment per night. Knowing (we would hope) that many students have a natural tendency to leave it all to Thursday night, they assign it anyway, in order to give students practice at planning ahead and budgeting time. This is an opportunity for parents and teachers to team up to teach children the disciplines of planning and budgeting. Elementary-school teachers who give weekly assignments without giving students techniques for planning and budgeting are irresponsible and setting some kids up for failure. Teachers who do not tell parents what their role is in supporting their students to learn these disciplines are missing an important opportunity.

There are disciplines for everything from doing homework to getting to school on time to washing the dishes. A host of disciplines will reveal themselves in the stories ahead, and I have focused not so much on classroom or home disciplines, but on the disciplines of leading one's genius out into the world.

Often more than one apply in a situation, so the disciplines don't nicely line up one by one with the stories. Perhaps it is best to read this book as a scavenger hunt: Can you find the disciplines embedded in the stories? I will flag some of them, but some I will not; you will have to find them yourselves or think up your own. Appendix A is a starter list of disciplines A-to-Z, with plenty of room to build your own list as you discover more.

One of the fascinating aspects of many of these disciplines is that they can be a little unnatural, countercultural, and, well, not normal. I have found that I must frequently remind people: "Don't do it the normal way. Do it the disciplined way."

**Disciplined behavior is not always normal behavior.**

If a parent says to me, "*We* had a little trouble with *our* homework last night," I know we have a problem of ownership that will undermine the student's performance. Parents need to remind themselves: "If we care more about something than the child does, we absolve the child of responsibility."

Facing and "leaning into" pain, disappointment, loss, and failure really do maximize learning and increase one's chances of success. Struggle strengthens so much more than success. But it takes discipline and practice to be empathetic of a child's problems without taking them on, or rescuing, trying to engineer success preemptively.

Trying to stay out of trouble actually causes a child to be in and out of trouble. It is a discipline to focus on the goal (learning, facing hard work, working out a conflict on your own) rather than avoiding "negative stuff."

One detailed anecdote *is* worth a thousand generalizations, but it takes practice to get in the habit of sticking to the facts, relating stories with details. It is all too natural to default to generalizations such as Armand is disruptive, Johnny is mean, Amelia is shy, Izzy is rambunctious. The discipline is to ask what Izzy's rambunctiousness looks like, or say "Tell me a story that will bring Johnny's meanness to life." For only with the details can we get to the thing that needs to change.

In her book *Mindset: The New Psychology of Success* Carol Dweck, a professor of psychology at Stanford University, summarizes years of research suggesting that in our ability-obsessed culture students perform better when they focus on learning and hard work rather than on intelligence and ability.[3] So we have to learn some counter-cultural behaviors. For instance when your child shows you a piece of work it is undisciplined to say: "My, how smart you are." Much better for us to think of something new like: "Oh, good, I can see you have been practicing" or "Did you work hard on it?"

Standards (which everybody seems to think are the savior of education these days) actually increase the measuring-up factor, which decreases a person's sense of his or her own authority and ultimately the quality of his or her performance and achievement. It takes discipline to remind the student and everyone working with the student to focus on setting their own goals, defining their own path to their own success to build their own sense of achievement in the context of standards without giving over the self to the standards.

It is normal to want our kids to be good, but in trying to be good, they often externalize the good and divide themselves into good self and bad self. We actually create Jekyll and Hyde-type people by using the language of "good" and "bad." It is a discipline to focus on integrity rather than goodness as we engage in the endless learning process of acquiring the toolbox of disciplines that help us merge our own inspiration with the requirements of the environment.

Trying to get another person to change without changing your own behavior or changing the context of your interaction will rarely work, but it is common. There are a whole set of disciplines that we need to learn in order to keep learning and not be a prisoner of however you finish this sentence: "I'm a believer in . . ."

I am sure most readers by now have turned to the list of disciplines in Appendix A. One caution: Any list like this reminds me of the time I came home from a conference of marriage counselors and showed my former wife a list of twenty-eight "rules for fair fighting." She read it carefully and said, "Yup. Everything I can't do when I am mad."

So an overarching principle of helping our children learn— and one of the most important—is the principle that we are often incapable of following the principles. Many years ago, after the funeral of one of my favorite uncles, I was confessing to my cousin how badly I thought I had messed up my children. She said, "Oh, Ricky, don't you know we all mess up our children? We can't help it. It's been set up that way."

She was right, of course. Each human being has strengths and weaknesses making it easier or harder for us to use certain disciplines. For example, most teachers are not equally good with all ages of children. Some teachers are great early-childhood educators but not so good at first grade. Some are naturally elementary teachers but not so good with middle-schoolers. Everyone knows that teaching middle school is a peculiar gift that only a few people have, and that most great high school teachers should not be teaching elementary school students. The day my daughter Lizzie got her multi-subject credential, I took her out to dinner to celebrate. (There are two Lizzie's in my life these days—a daughter and a step-daughter.) During the conversation, I asked her what grades she was looking forward to teaching.

She said without hesitation, "Kindergarten, first, second, and fifth."

"Huh," I said. "That's funny. What about third and fourth?"

"I don't think I would be good with them."

"Why not?"

"I don't understand their humor."

If there are very few teachers who can be good with all ages, how can we expect parents to be good with their children at every age? Parents have similarly disparate emotional and intellectual makeups that make them better or worse with different ages. My son, Peter, was terribly upset with himself in the first year of his son's life: "I just can't relate to him." He felt like he didn't love his son, Elijah. All this changed in Eli's second year of life, so that by age two Peter couldn't get enough of his son. He was brilliant at playing with him and holding him accountable and setting boundaries all at the same time. Eli's mother, who was equally brilliant in the first year of her son's life, found Eli very frustrating by age two.

On top of this, each of us, each parent and each child, is dynamic, not static, and therefore so is the relationship. We have a natural tendency to think of our children and ourselves as being "a certain way," and assume that the resulting relationship is more or less the way it will always be. It is a discipline to remind ourselves that things change and to give this change some time and space to happen. As our children move from age five to twenty-two, we have to move from being good kindergarten-teacher types to good first-grade-teacher types to good fifth-grade-teacher types to good seventh-grade-teacher types to good . . . *Stop.* Stop trying to be a teacher. Just take your young adult out for a cup of coffee and let her talk.

This is why no two siblings are being raised in the same family. The parents that raised my older brother were different parents from the ones who raised me, and our two younger siblings were raised in a completely different family of six than the tiny family of four that my older brother and I grew up in.

So, yes, there is a science of education represented by the principles embedded in Appendix A. The miserable truth is, however, that when we are in the kitchen trying to get dinner ready, and we have a frying pan in one hand and are trying to adjust the flame on the stove with the other, and Francis has just messed up the table that Freda was so carefully setting and has started to chase her around the kitchen, it is very hard to remember: "U. Find the right words. (Don't just repeat or say the wrong ones louder.)"

Therefore, acquisition of the disciplines of the science of education requires practicing some spiritual disciplines, disciplines we might call habits of the heart: patience, perseverance, courage, and humor.

# 3.

# Education

We commonly think of "educating" as something we do to someone else, but that understanding is essentially backward. Education is leading, not directing. Education is leading the genius out into the world to function effectively and gracefully within it. Doing something *to* anyone is not education. Mobilizing the student's genius, their inner authority, their teacher within, is critical for the success of the enterprise. Genius is the engine of education and the taproot of our learning.

A great and very experienced first-grade teacher I know likes to say, "I don't teach kids to read; they teach themselves." If you actually saw all the work that she puts into carefully planning what the students will do every day, your first reaction would be: "How can you say that? You are obviously teaching them how to read. Just look at all the things you are doing to get them to read."

But if you were to ask her that question, she would respond: "I am creating the conditions for reading to take place. Each student is doing it on his or her own. For some students, it happens effortlessly over the summer, and the parents couldn't say how they did it. For others it is relatively easy for them to learn phonics, and they move quickly from sounding out words to just recognizing them; for others; no amount of phonics will do the trick, because their brains just don't work that way. For some students, it is a struggle that lasts for years, as their brains are forced to organize in a way that is not natural for them. They do it on their own because they *have* to do it on their own."

In a world filled with the written word, they are naturally motivated to read, and they will try. They have to teach themselves to read, because it is their unique brains that will be doing it, which will have to organize themselves in their own ways.

Another important point is that reading is not a superficial skill. Reading is an act that involves the whole body and soul. Lucy Calkins, a professor of education at Columbia University's Teachers College, says that reading and writing are the same process, rather than opposite processes (input and output). Reading and writing are both acts of meaning creation.[4] If we understand that this thirst for meaning is driven by the genius trying to make its way in the world, we are better able to help our children. We become involved in our children's education, not just the acquisition of a few skills.

Parents started worrying about Jonathan in first grade, because he was not taking to reading. He struggled with phonics, and by second grade was actually avoiding the written word because it was not fun. The second-grade teacher followed the first-grade teacher in trying to help his parents not to worry but instead to simply read to him at home and to be patient. By third grade, they had decided that they were being irresponsible parents and that we were not addressing his "problem." They got Jonathan tested by a learning-skills specialist, who diagnosed him as "dyslexic"; they hired a tutor, who worked with him one hour a week. Meanwhile, the third-grade teacher kept focusing the curriculum and the energy of the students on matters of high intellectual interest. Although Jonathan continued to avoid books and to struggle when the teacher or the tutor forced him to decode words and to read a sentence out loud, he was one of the leaders in the class when it came to discussing the culture of the Ohlone Indians (a local native tribe); the social, racial, and religious conflicts in the California missions; and the lives and habits of spiders and insects. By eighth grade Jonathan was a reader. Keeping him focused on intellectual challenges he could be enthusiastic about was essential.

Dyslexia is not a disease. It is not even a condition. Dyslexia means "trouble reading," and under its large umbrella are grouped a wide range of neurological configurations in a wide variety of minds. Sure, when specialists declare, "Yes, your child has dyslexia," they are saying that your child's mind has trouble with some things that other minds do easily, like seeing the difference between *b* and *d*.

However, while it may be true that all dyslexics are similar, it is also true that no two dyslexics are alike. Eden, for instance, stumbles as she proceeds through the letters of a word, trying to sound out the syllables and turn that string of letters into a word. Aiden can do that just fine, if he slows down, but naturally gravitates to reading the first letter and guesses the rest of the word from the context. Eddie, in the fourth grade, can get through reading a passage aloud accurately and fluently, but can only answer about 50 percent of the questions about the passage accurately. Abby reads through the same passage slowly, adding an "eh" sound at the end of a number of words, as if there were an extra syllable. It seems to take her forever to get through the passage, but she can not only answer all the questions about the passage accurately but can also elaborate and tell you many of her own thoughts on the subject. All four have been "diagnosed" as dyslexic.

Teaching any of the academic disciplines takes a lot of doing, but underlying all that activity, with or without tutors, must be the understanding that the development of these skills is in the service of, and concurrent with, the engagement of genius. Teaching academics in a spiritual, emotional, and intellectual vacuum will not work for most children. If that method seems to work for some children, it is because reading itself comes easily to them, and reading has become a vehicle for the liberation of genius. If this engagement has not occurred, then all the activity was mostly for naught.

# 4.

# Character, Integrity, and Virtue

Another manifestation of genius is character, and so education is all about character. To the Greeks, *kharakter* was the imprint that the gods put on the soul at birth. Educating is creating the conditions in which the character that is your child becomes what he or she is supposed to become. Making our way in the world is a process of creation, and our character is what we are creating. Integrity is our compass, and virtues are disciplines for acting with integrity, so we can be true to ourselves in a challenging, ever-changing world.

But today character is another word at risk of becoming divorced from its original meaning. It has already split in two: character meaning a unique person (and a bit weird), as in "he's a real character"; and character meaning a moral fiber, as in "he is a person of good character." For the purposes of education, we need the original, because it includes both. The goal of education is for a person to be **1)** comfortable in his own skin as **2)** that skin struggles to keep harmonizing itself with a challenging and changing world.

One day at school, Helen, age three, sat in the sandbox scooping sand into a bucket with a bright green scooper. Her teacher came by and said (as a good teacher would), "So, Helen, how many scoops do you think it will take to fill up your bucket?"

Helen, strawberry blond hair flaming on this windy day, looked up from her work and said in a friendly, matter-of-fact way: "Miss Alicia, why don't you go teach those two kids over there?" What a character.

These are the moments we must keep. We must ponder them in our hearts. If we must keep a journal about our children, these events are what should be in it. Recording at what age they learned to crawl or walk or talk or read shrinks to insignificance in the face of such character-revealing moments.

I told Helen's parents this story, and the next Monday they emailed me another Helen story:

*Helen was again playing in the sandbox over the weekend. On the other side, a brawl broke out between a brother and sister. Helen looked as they knocked each other to the ground, arguing over a shovel. She watched intently for a while, then calmly looked around, found two more shovels, walked over, and handed one to each of the siblings. The fighting stopped. They handed Helen the shovel they had been fighting over and went back to playing happily together. No words were exchanged.*

Helen's parents reported their happiness that she had acquired some very important skills. They noticed that Helen had observed a conflict, deciphered the dynamic, figured out a solution, and implemented that solution, all with the utmost confidence. Indeed, the skills Helen practiced are the kind necessary for success and satisfaction in the maelstrom of life that will be coming at her in ever-increasing degrees of complexity for the rest of her life.

**Character-building is self-fulfillment.**

Helen's parents are wise enough to know that these sandbox skills will stand her in good stead both in the classroom, when she is confronted with academic problems, and also in future social situations. Whether she finds herself later in life raising her own children or resolving conflicts between Israelis and Palestinians, or anything, she not only has some of the critical disciplines necessary to make of herself all that she is meant to be, but is also capable of creating conditions in which others are also safe to be themselves.

However, let us not lose focus. The confidence with which Helen played Helen is what matters most. Her constructive impact on her environment both resulted from and justified this confidence. Happiness, success, winning, and achievement are not what we should wish for our children but the confidence to live in life's tensions—the confidence to learn from disappointment, failure, losing, and flops. When a person is fully herself, she is also doing her best to harmonize herself with her environment. When I was a little boy and behaving badly, my mother would often say: "Ricky, you are not yourself today."

**Integrity**

When a person is fully herself, she is integrating all the impulses and drives inside her in a way which is constructive in her environment. This is the essence of integrity—wholeness which includes what's good for both self and other. But again our culture has distorted our thinking in ways which are unhelpful for bringing out the best in people. The dictionary on my computer gives three definitions: "1. the quality of possessing and steadfastly adhering to high moral principles or professional standards 2. the state of being complete or undivided (formal) 3. the state of being sound or undamaged (formal)."

When using the word integrity, it is important to hold all three meanings of the word at once. Helen's integrity in this novel situation caused peace to break out in the sandbox. When our genius is engaged and our character is manifest, we are **a)** sound and undamaged, **b)** complete and undivided, and **c)** moral. This is integrity.

Helen was playing out of her head. She was not trying to be good or moral. She was not trying to impress her parents. She was simply being herself. Delighting in the character of a child not only helps the child, but it can make the world a better place. Often children make bad decisions—or no decision at all—they just react. In these situations, the adults need to do two things at once: **1)** make sure the environment says "No" clearly and accurately and **2)** teach the empowering discipline.

## Virtue

Virtue is usually understood as being good, but this undercuts the usefulness of virtues. Some virtues like justice, joy, grace, and compassion are evidence of character in action and therefore best seen as aspirations. Most virtues, however, are better seen as disciplines—tools we are trained to use effectively for the full development of our character, rather than goods that we must sacrifice ourselves to attain. Faith, hope, charity, and love are disciplines, for instance. Tough situation? Put yourself in a faithful, hopeful, loving frame of mind and you will be at your best. Treating the other person with charity usually produces better results all around. It is better to teach these virtues as skills rather than to advocate for them as values. Courage, patience, perseverance, authorship, authenticity, mindfulness, awareness, and tolerance are all disciplines for developing and strengthening character.

Just as integrity is the core of being oneself successfully in the world (including being in harmony with the needs and demands of the world), so also having character is most fundamentally about being true to oneself, with the understanding that one cannot be true to oneself if one is false to others. Unfortunately, so much of "character education" seems to be about trying to impose goodness on children, rather than guiding them to apply themselves gracefully and uniquely in the world.

Therefore, the end of education is not "character," but characters; for our goal is not to turn out people "of good character," but people who are good at being their own unique character. There are as many different characters in the world as there are people, and education should produce heterogeneity, not homogeneity. I use genius and character interchangeably, as they manifest slightly different aspects of the same thing: that someone who is becoming.

Remembering that education is leading character into the world to function gracefully within it helps us to keep our eye on the right ball. It can remind us that our children need to be noticed more and analyzed less, delighted in more than worried over, challenged more than protected, not so much made to be good as taught to be good at being themselves. This focus helps us to play position and to let our children struggle. It shows us the folly of labeling, helps us deal with demons and monsters, and reminds us that we are dealing with an infinite mystery. It reminds us that we need to open ourselves up to our own learning. Believe in your child's character, and study it with your heart.

Focusing on our own education as we struggle with theirs is as much for our own benefit, joy, and well-being as for our children's. Our own education may feel like a secondary responsibility, but it is at least as important. Keeping our focus on the child's genius forces us to grow in our own integrity, our own virtuous practice, and the development of our own character. We will be more effective that way.

# 5.

# Air-Traffic Controller

In 1955—twelve years before Brooke took her walk—when I was in fifth grade, back before there were such things as "playdates," my main activity—with or without a friend—was hiking off into the Connecticut woods. All that was involved in launching such "expotitions," as Winnie the Pooh would say, was for one of us kids to yell up to our moms, "We're going on a hike." The reply was always, "Okay. Be back for dinner," and we were off.

Adventuring into unknown territory was one of my favorite pastimes, and perhaps one of the most important elements of my education. By the time my friends and I were twelve, bicycles were widening our horizons. My mother, who had four of us to keep track of, was more relieved than worried that I was out on my own. She was like an air-traffic controller, launching four children and a husband into the world every morning and watching each of us circle back to what she hoped would be three-point landings every evening. Then we would sit together at her table and be a family.

Of course, she learned early on that with five loved ones to watch over and worry about, it was a mathematical probability that she could expect at least one of us to be "coming in on a wing and a prayer." With me, it was usually bloody knees, but sometimes my mother dealt with bloody heads as well. From the perspective of us kids, a wound was always a badge of honor, proof of something—worthiness. Yes, worthiness, though with or without the blood, these adventures were always some kind of triumph.

Though we never talked about it, I know now, looking back, that my mother, managing all those loved ones and trying to have a life of her own, often experienced psychic overload and went numb. (She could not allow herself to get mad; neither she nor I got good training in how to handle anger. Anger was evil, end of story.) Her relief, therefore, at having us go out the doorway, though subtly expressed, was strong enough for me to feel. I did not consciously register the nearly mechanical way she would get dinner on the table then, but fifty years later, I can tell that it settled firmly into my psyche. Now, when I remember her saying, "I just want to curl up with a good book," I realize how draining the sustained attention to her five loves, those five responsibilities, those five pains in the neck, must have been. Being an air-traffic controller is intense work. Parenting is even tougher.

Kids watch parents out of the corner of one eye. They are focused on their own business, a business that comes from within and is the result of many forces, interior and exterior. So all kids are badly in need of air-traffic controllers, because there is just too much to worry about, given those impulses from within and pressures from without. When they say, "Mom! No!" or complain, "Oh, Dad," it is usually not because their parents are wrong, or even that they think their parents are wrong. It is because parental imposition is just one thing too many. This extra, additional variable that parents lay on children threatens to throw them off course, a course they would rather not have to correct. "It's nice to have a parent in the conning tower, but she doesn't seem to realize what's involved in flying this damned crate. She just has no idea of the pressures I am under! *Sigh!*"

Back in 1955, the role of air-traffic controller was played predominantly by the mother. In some circles, it was even bad form for a mother to try to raise a child and work outside the home at the same time. (Even twenty-five years later, when it is expected that women will pursue careers, the mother is usually still the air-traffic controller.) My father, along with the vast majority of husbands, saw his role as bringing home the bacon. He felt strongly—even self-righteous—about this. His wife should and must focus on making a home for the whole family, including, but by no means limited to, the children.

Wanting to lead her own life (she *did* go to college, after all) and feeling the burden of taking responsibility for our lives as well, she was relieved when any one of us could take care of him or herself. From feeding myself (a big step forward) through doing my homework on my own and getting into college, the more I took responsibility, the more time she had for others and herself. I remember one dramatic moment in the hallway outside her bedroom when I said, "Mom ..." and got the annoyed response, "Can't I even go to the bathroom?!"

"Of course," I said. "You could have just told me." (And I wondered why it wasn't just that simple.)

A generation later, when I was looking after Brooke on that Saturday morning in 1967, I wanted my child to be able to take care of herself in the world. Just as I wanted Brooke to be self-motivated, self-directed, and self-sustaining for her own sake, I also wanted these things for my own reasons. I wanted to be able to pursue my life, too. I loved my daughter. I delighted in her, loved playing with her, and found her growth and development a never-ending, jaw-dropping source of amazement. On the other hand, she was not my work in the world. I was a teacher at the time, and though I did not then know that education would be my calling, I knew I was supposed to have some life and somehow make something of myself. I knew that being the air-traffic controller for my children was not it.

Between the blossoming of my independence at age ten and Brooke's birth when I was twenty-one, I must have gone on hundreds of adventures. The longer the radius of my world, the happier both my parents were. And between the ages of ten and twenty-one I faced many dangers. There was the time I found myself most of the way up a forty-foot cliff with no more toeholds to take up and no apparent way of going back down. There was the time I almost ran the boat aground in Narragansett Bay in the middle of the night. There was the time I dodged a truck and ran my Volkswagen off the edge of a bridge in the hills of eastern Kentucky.

For every near-death experience, I avoided a dozen perils. This makes well over a hundred things that my mother should have worried about, and I am sure she did. Nonetheless, she seemed to exude confidence that I could take care of myself in the world. Even when driving a car made the probabilities of death, homicide, or dismemberment much higher, I was not aware that my parents worried much.

It must have taken a lot of discipline on their part. However, I now suspect that it was not pure discipline. Having one more offspring off into the world was part of my parents' selfish wish fulfillment of hav-ing fewer blips on the radar screen. Often, taking care of yourself is also good parenting.

**Often, taking care of yourself is also good parenting.**

There are not many parents today who see themselves this way—or if they do, they keep it well hidden. Parents I know seem more like helicopters than air-traffic controllers.

They hover. Hovering is perhaps normal these days, but it often unknowingly stifles, inhibits, and in many ways is counterproductive to the discovery and development of a child's genius.

To be sure, "parent involvement" is a good thing. However, the question is not "Involvement: more or less?" but "What will be the *quality* of my involvement?" Parents must ask themselves, "Why am I paying attention? Are these my needs or my child's? Who is taking responsibility for what?" In the course of my career, as I have watched parents undermining their children's self-confidence and undercutting their effectiveness, I have developed Ackerly's First Law: When a parent takes responsibility for something in the child's realm (getting to school on time, homework, the capabilities of his body, what he is going to do with his life, etc.), it tends to absolve the child of responsibility for it.

# 6.

# Getting Our Children to Talk

∽

"How was school today?"

"Fine."

"What did you do?"

"Stuff."

Parents often complain that they can't get their children to talk about what went on in school. Others feel lucky that they "have one who likes to share their experience," but the former is much more common.

When our children go off to school, responsibility must progressively shift from parents to students, so that children will increasingly take responsibility for their own education. Ownership is *the* main predictor of success. This taking of responsibility happens quite naturally. When they walk in the gate of the school, they enter another country, a world of their own; it's a natural process.

The boundary between their two countries can be more or less permeable, and if home and school both play their cards right, it can be quite a friendly border, which is usually the case. But that doesn't mean the boundary ever goes away, nor should it. It is quite fair for children to say in their own way, "Mom,

Dad, this is my world; do not intrude." When I was raising two girls in New York, ages ago, our small apartment had one and a half bathrooms. At the beginning of second grade, my daughter, Lizzie, wrote two signs and put one on each door: One said KIDS, and the other said GROANUPS.

One of the most important jobs we have as parents is to let our children go off to school and let it be their own school. This is not to say that parents should stay away or shouldn't get involved or shouldn't ask questions about what goes on on the other side of those walls. The boundary is not a physical boundary, but a psychological one. This separation is both real and symbolic when parents come to a school assembly. The children sit with their classes, and parents stand around the outside. Parents and students come to the same assembly, and we all experience the same phenomena. It's just that the students in their circles are in a different world than the adults around the outside are. It all happens so naturally. Most of us, most of the time, honor the two worlds deep down without even thinking

**The boundary is not a physical boundary, but a psychological one.**

Some students are talkers; some are not so good with words. Some want to share; others have a strong need to keep their own worlds to themselves. Each of us needs a place of our own, into which others should not pry. Nevertheless, this does not mean that communication between the two worlds needs to break down—in fact, it must not. As they approach the teen years, children will want to say in a variety of ways, "Get out of my life." Parents must brace themselves for that message and accept it willingly; at the same time, we must not take it literally and totally. It is a statement about a shift in emphasis. They actually need and want us to be in their lives even more deeply; they just want us to do it in new ways, ways that reflect their higher level of maturity and competence.

Communication between these two worlds can be facilitated by specificity. Teachers should send home newsletters, or put what they are studying on the website, or do something to communicate directly to parents what's going on, so that parents are not in the dark. The purpose of these communications, however, is not for parents to take responsibility in the student's sphere of responsibility, but to help parents add specificity to their questions. If you know what's going on this week, you can come up with clever questions:

"What did you notice about caterpillars today?
"Which math center did you work in today?"
"Did you get a new book today?"
"Oh, so you finished *Puddles*. How did it end?"
"What did you learn about seeds today?"

You might get really clever and make a statement, instead of a question: "Hey, look! A pattern!" (You'll be helping us teach algebra without actually looking like you are being a teacher.) Compared to specific questions like those above, "What was the best thing that happened at school today?" seems rather pedestrian, but that's okay. Some parents have found that this question works quite well, too.

Getting our children to talk about their world is an art, not a science. Part of the art is a matter of timing. Maybe "How was school today?" is not only not the best line, but also perhaps not the question to pop the moment the child is climbing into the car. Maybe on the way to school in the morning is a better time to ask, "What are you looking forward to today?" That might give you something to talk about over dinner.

# 7.

# Making Them Strong, Letting Them Go

A parent of a sixth-grader stopped me in the hallway just after school one day to say that Sally, one of her daughters, had been unfairly marked tardy. "How could she have been late to class?" she asked. "We got here early this morning. I came into the building because I had to take care of some business in the office. I know we were on time."

I checked and found out that Sally had in fact shown up to class late. Maybe "we" had gotten to school on time, but Sally had not. When the mother and I spoke about it, I was sympathetic, but I reminded her that this was an opportunity to let her child take responsibility for getting to school on time.

"It will be a good thing to talk with her about," I said. "Remember to ask yourself, 'Whose problem is it?' At this age, you want her to take responsibility for getting to class on time. You can do your part, but you want her to care about it more than you do. Your job is only to drive the car. By contrast, some kids are so intent on not being late that they harass their parents to hurry up and not make them late. That could be your vision."

We have to keep our eye on the right ball: We are trying to raise independent people, people who can do things on their own, who take responsibility for creating lives they want to live.

When our children are new, we try to mold family life, including the children's behavior, into being the way we want it. By the time our children enter kindergarten, we have done so much training that children are hard-wired with our values: Be careful crossing streets, be nice to your little sister, be gentle with the dog, go to bed at eight, don't bother me while I am cooking—you could make a list of a hundred messages you have been trying to get across. Before age five, children really want to know what the formula for success is, and they sponge it up from us. They copy, practice, and test reality to identify what's real.

By the time they are five or so, though, a change occurs, and it is time for us to shift gears. If children are not doing what we want them to do, it is usually not because they don't know what we want—it is something else. Maybe they want to see if we really mean it. Maybe they want to see if other things work, too. Maybe they have trouble doing it or need practice or reminding. Maybe they want to see for themselves if it's really true. The more truths they find out for themselves, the better off they will be.

The elementary years are good ones, during which we can encourage our children to take on higher and higher levels of responsibility: for themselves, their work, their families, their communities, and their environment. The greater the sense of discipline that is internalized by the time they reach adolescence, the easier it will be for us to play our position, which should be more "coach" than "manager."

In the December 2004 issue of *Psychology Today* is an important article by Hara Estroff Marano, entitled "A Nation of Wimps"—required reading for all adults working with school-children.[5] It states that American parents are increasingly anxious about their children's success, and that because of this anxiety, they seem to be acting according to the theory that "nothing succeeds like success." Therefore, the parent who cares will hover, overplan, overprogram, overprotect, and act so as to engineer his child's success. The author cites a great deal of research that demonstrates the disastrous folly of this approach. Marano's article would be a wonderful starting place for a good reading list of experts who see disaster in hovering: David Elkind,[6] David Anderegg,[7] William Doherty and Barbara Carlson,[8] and Jerome Kagan.[9]

**Failure is at least as powerful an educator as success.**

Normally, parents and teachers act according to a theory that praise and success are the important active ingredients. The truth is that nothing succeeds like taking responsibility. Nothing succeeds like failure. Failure is at least as powerful an educator as success.

Success results from self-confidence, and self-confidence is built by a high incidence of turning a desire into a goal, a goal into a plan, and then persevering. Success that strengthens is success that meets one's own standards, not someone else's. Praise can feel good, but heavy doses of it can actually weaken self-confidence, since building self-confidence is placed in the hands of others. A prominent East Bay psychologist, Sheri Glucoft Wong, is famous for saying in her talks to parents, "Strengthen the child's disappointment muscle."[10]

I know I was probably irritating to Sally's mother when she spoke to me about her daughter's tardiness (or lack of tardiness), but the sixth-grader who wants to have a perfect attendance record has a fine opportunity to learn something because she is motivated, and we should not preempt it by taking it on. At her age, it is not important that she achieve a perfect record of being on time to class, but that she learn from the challenges of trying to achieve a perfect record. This is one way of showing that we believe in her genius.

# 8.

# Mr. Rick, Air-Traffic Controller

∽

When I look back on what I have made of myself, I see that I have been fathering for more than forty years—not just my own children, but other people's as well. It has been many things, but it has mainly been an education. (Brooke, the eldest, will turn 44 this year. Peter is 39, Lizzie 32, and Katie 28.) Seven years after Brooke went for her walk, I became the principal of a private school in Kansas City, Missouri. Many years later, a parent from this school with whom I was reminiscing said, "I will always have this image of you on the first day of school, walking those hallways with the twelve-foot ceilings with one crying three-year-old on each hip." As I think back on it, I realize that I have helped to father thousands of children.

In addition to being the father of other people's children, in recent years I have become a grandparent. When, at the age of fifty-seven, I became headmaster of my fourth school—a school with three-year-olds, thirteen-year-olds, big trees, two sheep, and six chickens in the middle of a big city—my name changed, too. Instead of Mr. Ackerly, I am now Mr. Rick. It was awkward for me at first. But I got used to it, partly because it sounded a little grandfatherly, and especially because Mr. Rick doesn't have to wear a coat and tie anymore.

As the teachers and parents at my school are more and more the ages of my own children, I find them sometimes relating to me as their father, not just the stand-in father of the students. Now, this is not how I see myself. I am just a guy, Mr. Rick, playing a role: school principal. The kids, of course, are the students; the adults (all of whom I view as teachers) are my colleagues and parent partners. But from time to time, surprised by a certain reaction I've gotten from a teacher or by an outburst from a certain parent, I realize they are not reacting so much to me in my role, but to some parent image they harbor inside themselves. So it seems that I am a quasi-father, pseudo-father, proto-father, stand-in father, and ersatz father.

Thousands of parents have entrusted me with the responsibility of watching over their children, keeping them safe and educating them. When they are ready, the children just walk out the doors of their homes or their cars, through the gate of my school, and onto my radar screen. I become the air-traffic controller for hundreds of people.

What did I do last week? I reminded a student that his friendship with that other girl is more important than being right, helped a teacher not get distracted by a parent's anger and focus on what is best for the child, helped a parent see that facing her fear about her child would make both the fear and the problem go away, helped a child see that taking responsibility for his conflict would fix the relationship, helped a teacher find the words to tell it like it is to a parent, and helped a parent find the courage to talk to another parent who was bothering her.

During the day, my radar screen is swarming with blips. It's exciting and tiring. At night, though, my radar screen functions differently. When I wake up at 4 A.M., it automatically turns on and gives me a printout of relationships at risk. Then, whether

I like it or not, I problem-solve. There are some conversations I have redone and rehearsed and redone again hundreds of times. They actually get better each time, and when it comes time for me to have those conversations in the pressure of the actual moment, I do better than I would have had I said what I had originally been considering. So the radar screen works well for me.

As air-traffic controller, I form partnerships with many other air-traffic controllers, and together we work to keep our children safe on their journeys. As partners, we play different roles based on our different authorities, which are themselves based on our different positions. Through triumph and tragedy, we learn together.

Here is a road map that a sixth-grade teacher, Susan Porter, and I came up with many years ago to define those different positions. She still hands this document out to parents at "Back-to-School Night" in September. Parents and teachers should get together and read it to one another once a year.

Defining the Parent-Teacher Contract

As the teacher, I can and will:
- care for your child and make sure she is safe
- praise her when she deserves it
- be on her case when it's necessary
- encourage her to find her strength and use it
- challenge her to use her weakness to improve it
- show her how to take charge of her learning
- be there for her when she needs extra help
- provide her with a wide variety of ideas, subjects, and activities

I cannot:
- love her as you do
- protect her from disappointment*
- make sure she is happy*
- make sure she is not bored*
- ensure she has friends*
- make sure she gets good grades*
- guarantee she will get into a good high school*
- give her self-respect or self-confidence or high self-esteem*

* These are what the student must do for herself.

As the parent, you can:
- know your child for who she is
- appreciate your child for who she is, not for who you hope she'll be
- be there to console her when she needs it
- listen to her in such a way that she feels listened to
- in listening, help her fight her own battles
- enjoy her
- delight in her
- have fun with her
- give her unconditional love and trust even when you don't feel it's justified
- believe in her even when your feelings tell you otherwise

You should not:
- feel guilty for your child's disappointing achievement or "poor" performance
- feel inadequate that you cannot respond to her every need on short notice
- compare your child to other students
- fight her battles for her

What being a parent and being a principal have in common is the necessity of making sure that we don't overplay our hands, that we don't get out of our positions and exercise too much or too little force in trying to get our children to behave as we want them to. Supporting the genius of each blip on our

**Our authority must increase the authority of our children.**

radar screen is about making sure the exercise of our authority increases the authority of our children. When we say no (and we should not shy away from saying no), we define reality for the child so that he can direct himself more productively. A child needs boundaries in order to self-direct more gracefully and effectively.

# II: Self Do It

.

# 9.

# Self Do It

∽

When my mother was seventy-five, she found herself alone. Even though she was a home manager with more than fifty years of experience and had spent the previous five years caring for my eighty-nine-year-old stepfather, she was strangely lost. What she faced the day he died was not so much being alone but anxiety—anxiety based on a vague sense that she couldn't manage. Being on her own was scary. Seeing her distress on the first day of my visit to her new home, I told her the story of how her granddaughter Katie had acquired the nickname "Self."

When Katie was between the ages of one and two, whenever people tried to help her do things like put on her coat, peel a banana, eat, or get into her car seat, she would resist quite firmly, saying, "Self do it." She did this so often that one day, a close friend of the family who happened to be visiting renamed Katie "Self." My mom loved the story, and for the last ten years of her life, whenever she got anxious about her own capabilities, she would say to herself, "Self do it."

This is the focus we need in raising children. We want them to feel capable of "Self do it" long before they reach the age of seventy-five. They will do so naturally, if we support them properly. Humans, including the youngest ones, have a natural inclination to be decision makers, to be Selves, and we adults play an important role as children experience their interdependence with the world in ever-widening circles of complexity. We have to do two things at once: push back when Self is not doing what the environment requires Self to do, and love each Self unconditionally as we are making our demands and saying no. But the engine that drives all of this is genius. Each young Self needs to trust his or her own genius. It surely helps a child gain this self-trust, if we believe there is such a genius.

One day, the parent of three-year-old Nicholas reported to me on how he had mastered what had seemed a continuous battle of wills with his little one. Every time an adult wanted Nicholas to do something, he would immediately try to turn the moment into a question of "Will you make me, or will I be able to continue doing whatever I want?" The father told me he remembered that I had said, "'Consequences' is not a euphemism for 'punishment.'" His first moment of success came when Nick had been dawdling about getting into the car. The father said, "Do you want to get into the car seat on your own, or do you want me to do it for you?"

When the dawdling continued, he said, "We need to leave in ten seconds. I will count out three seconds, and if you are not in your seat, I will do it for you, and then next time you can show me you can do it on your own."

This time, of course, he had to put Nicholas in the seat. This involved violent protest that included screaming and crying, but my friend never had to put his son in the car seat again. For a while he had to ask Nicholas the question about whether he was ready to take on the responsibility, and sometimes he had to set a time limit and start counting, but from then on Nicholas did it on his own.

When I watch first-grade girls on the playground, they seem

so mature. Something about their language, the way they negotiate with one another, and their bearing makes them seem like young women. One day while on the playground waiting for school to start, I observed Alana approach first-grade teacher Kathy to complain that Rebecca had called her a name. Kathy asked, "Did you tell her you didn't like it?" When Alana answered no, Kathy suggested that she do so. Kathy and I saw the resulting interaction from a distance. Alana frowned, and her hands rotated in front of her as she talked. Rebecca studied Alana as she listened, then, with a sincere expression on her face, said something. The smiles came back to the girls' faces, and they returned to playing together. "Self do it."

As teachers and parents get more and more experienced, we learn just how and when to intervene. Just as it was less important for Katie to get her coat on than to show that she could do it on her own, so it was less important that the conflict get resolved than for Alana to learn how to resolve her own social problems. Kathy was teaching one of the disciplines of conflict resolution—the first rule: Face your antagonist. "Self" will naturally "do it." The jargon for this process is "individuation." Our role is counter-intuitive: supporting self by defining boundaries.

Years ago, George, the teacher in charge of our service learning programs, came to my office more distraught than I had ever seen this calm, centered man. His scalp glistening pink, he said: "We have been kicked out of the Youth Mentoring Program."

"What do you mean?"

George launched into the full story about how Elliott, a seventh-grade boy who was new to the school, had misbehaved so badly at the mentoring center that the organizers removed our whole school from the program, forbidding us to return. George sat in the chair opposite me with his head in his hands and said: "Nothing like this has ever happened before. This is the worst moment in my career. It is so embarrassing."

I said, "Talk to the organizers and find out if there were any conditions under which they would allow us to return. I will talk to Elliott."

When I asked Elliott what he had done, he gave me a lot of I-was-only, and other-people-were-too. I told him that one of the consequences of his actions was that our school was not welcome back at the Youth Mentoring Program. He seemed bothered and surprised by that, but continued to be defensive. I said, "Elliott, you have gotten us kicked out of one of the most important things that we do. You have taken a program that we are proud of and ruined it for yourself, your classmates, and the school. You have to figure out how you are going to fix this."

"But what can I do?" asked Elliott.

"I don't know. That is for you to figure out. This is very important. When you go home tonight, you think about it. When you have a plan, I want you to come back and tell me about it. Meanwhile, don't come back. Stay home. You can't be in this school until you fix this problem." (I did not use the word "suspension"; my focus is always on increasing responsibility, never punishment.)

Elliott's parents called me that night to try to tell me that the punishment did not fit the crime. He had just been fooling around; he was just being a kid; he was only thirteen, after all; what about the others? I said they should come in the following morning—without Elliott—so we could talk. Luckily, in the ensuing conference it did not take these parents long to see what I was trying to do, and that I saw this as a chance for Elliott to grow up a little more by facing the consequences of his actions.

Elliott was out the rest of the day. When he came to my office two days later, the first thing he said was, "No one else can fix this but me, can they?"

"No," I said. "Only you."

"Do you think they would let me come talk to them?"

"I don't know. Would you like me to help you find out?"

"Yes."

I picked up the phone and called the director of the Youth Mentoring Program and told her that Elliott wanted to come talk to her. She was reluctant, not wanting to spend her time on children for whom other people were responsible, but she relented after I convinced her of Elliott's sincerity.

I drove Elliott downtown. He went in the door on his own, he went in the office on his own, he got himself back into the program on his own, and he got the school back in. "Self do it."

What these incidents have in common is that success came from adults acting as if they believe in the child. When we trust Self to do it, we trust in something beyond what is obvious from the behavior that is before us. We trust in the child's genius, her calling, his character, that inner voice that guides and directs.

Almost every year, I hear stories from my high school colleagues about kids who get into trouble and parents who come to the rescue. Rather than letting the kids "take their punishments," these parents bring in lawyers to defend the students, because they want to make sure the episode doesn't go "on their records." They have their eye on the wrong ball, and in each case I am willing to bet that this isn't the first time the parents have failed to hold their child accountable for his or her mistakes.

When we feel conflicted about how best to approach one of these difficult situations, a good discipline to remember is "Self do it." Children will show us what they are ready for, and we can follow their lead.

Never pass up an opportunity to let children show you their stuff. They love to do this. Ever notice how kids ask questions by telling you things like "Salamanders don't have babies, they lay eggs," "Mountain lions eat children," "Johnny is dirty—his skin is brown," and "God is a woman"? It seems that they give us millions of such statements a day. It is not that they actually know so much; rather, it's that they want to know so much. If we see kids as driven by Self to know, we can hear all these claims properly. They are saying, "Dad, tell me all you know about salamanders, lions, skin color, or God."

Raising self-disciplined young people is infinitely complex; there are many pressures at work in the millions of teachable moments life affords us. And when faced with these millions of opportunities—"Do your homework"; "Don't talk that way to your little brother"; "Clean up your room"—parents don't need to feel that there is only one right way to handle them. To intervene or let it be? To fix the problem or back off? Teachers and parents face hundreds of such dilemmas. As we move from situation to situation, we have to keep the central background question in view: "Whose journey is this?"

The art of playing position is the art of being responsible without being in control, the art of collaboration and shared decision-making. It's paradoxical. To maximize someone else's education, we need to treat that person as if she knows what she is doing (even though we know that she may not). We make a mistake every time we take responsibility for something that children can handle themselves. At the same time, "backing off" is not good parenting. Children need us to be more involved in their lives, not less. They need us to take responsibility at times when it is our turn. They need us to play position.

My wife, Victoria, likes to say, "Each of us is starring in his or her own drama." Whether it is a comedy or a tragedy, we need to define the role we will play in it. Each child is on a journey guided by his or her genius, and we need to find our place on each child's journey, just as our parents found their place in ours.

# 10.

# Boundary-Setting

Parents continue to find boundary-setting challenging. A working mother sent me this question recently:

*When a working mom encounters a new behavior problem she has to figure out how to handle this issue at home. My question is: How should she work with other caregivers on the issue? Many children may have multiple caregivers during the day. Maybe the child goes to kindergarten, then to an after-school day-care program, and spends many Saturdays with Grandma. Is it important to talk to each caregiver about how everyone is handling this new behavior problem? What if the mom decides to do timeouts at home but the other caregivers do not provide the same consequence? Maybe Grandma laughs it off. Should a parent discuss discipline with teachers or a nanny at the start of a new child-care situation? What kinds of conversations should these be?*

These wonderful questions brought to mind a tragedy of errors resulting in the rapid deterioration of Keith's behavior in kindergarten and the relatively simple way of getting Keith back on track. It's a story about how easy and natural it is for boundaries to get blurred, communication muddled, and authorities to become confused. It also points to the possibility that parents, teachers, and other caregivers can prevent a lot of bad behavior by collaborative boundary-setting.

Keith is one of those five-year-old boys who runs onto the yard the first day of school, a big smile on his face, looking for friends, action, and a chance to exercise his physical and intellectual prowess. He is the kind of kid great kindergarten teachers love, and rookies think they love until they are confronted with disobedience.

Early on, Keith established friendships with two other rambunctious boys, and before long they were a gang who cared more about impressing one another with their brilliance than doing what the teacher wanted. Their arrogance got to the point that by October, they would even tell the teacher what was right and wrong. One of the other boys even gave instructions to teachers, as if he had gone to graduate school and knew what was supposed to happen.

Keith tried that with me. I was so surprised, I got mad at him. (It would have been more effective to have been matter-of-fact and stern, brow closing down above squinting eyes, as I said: "No. You need to do it my way, and you need to do it the teacher's way. You are sounding very arrogant. Do you know what arrogance means?" Then, after a brief pause: "We will talk about arrogance first thing in the morning.")

The teacher decided (but wouldn't say) that the students' apparent arrogance was, of course, the result of their having grown up in affluent, arrogant families where their parents would let them run things at home like little princes. She began sending them to the principal's office. This had the effect of shutting down the disobedient behavior in the moment but not eliminating the fundamental problem.

Under these conditions, Keith's behavior alternated between

good and bad. When his mother picked him up at the end of the day, the teacher would make a short report through the window of the car—well, not exactly a report, unless you call "Keith had a hard day" or "Keith was sent to the principal's office" a report.

His parents were terribly disturbed. Their wonderful boy was becoming a "bad kid." On their own, they established consequences at home. Every day things went "badly" at school, there would be one. They even (quite cleverly) had him start his own 'book of consequences.' For each bad behavior (like interrupting or hitting), Keith would write the word at the top of the left-hand page, draw a picture of the offense in action, and at the top of the opposite page write what the consequence would be (going to bed early, being confined to his room until dinner, no TV) and draw a picture of that as well.

This was great educational activity: really good parents supporting the teacher and the school. One big problem, however: Keith was beginning to develop a self-image as a troublemaker.

The parents and the teachers thought they were cooperating well, but their cooperation was flawed. They were each operating independently, linked only through the window of the car at dismissal time. Keith was getting double jeopardy. He would be punished at school, and then, when he ran to the car at the end of the day, all smiles and ready for hugs, he was greeted with a distressed mom who had just discovered that she would have to "discipline" him. They drove home almost every day in hell—dread spilling out of open windows on a sunny day, and fear stifling the atmosphere in the car on rainy days.

As it turned out, the solution was easy and a little counterintuitive. Parents and teachers agreed on a plan. The book was good. He would maintain and develop it at school, not at home. Consequences for bad behavior at school would occur at school only, not at home. Consequences for bad behavior at home would occur at home, and not be communicated to school. Reports between school and home would be more detailed, less emotional . . . and sent by e-mail . . . and just FYI. Only friendly good-byes and hellos at dismissal time.

As soon as this new order was established, the bad behavior went away. Completely! The very next day! Keith's parents reported to me that it was like a miracle: a sudden and complete fixing of the problem. Keith went back to being the delightful, brilliant, rambunctious boy who made others laugh and shone in class with his thoughtful comments and starred on the playground whenever a ball was involved.

There were many dynamics going on in this situation—situations like this are usually quite complex—but whenever we achieve success, we should ask ourselves, "What did we do right?" A starting point is to recognize that this is another case of a child feeling surrounded: "Teachers at school, teachers at home, everywhere I look, teachers." Giving these very responsible parents the permission just to be parents and not to feel they had to pick up where the teacher left off was the first step.

Second, when a person, especially a child, makes a mistake or does something wrong, yes, they need to experience a consequence—they need to repair the damage they have done—but then they need to move on. They need forgiveness. If the mistake occurs at school, the problem is between the student and the teacher, and the teacher and student should fix the problem; that should be the end of it. When the teacher told the parent that Keith had misbehaved, she failed to also pass on the forgiveness.

Thirdly, Keith was focusing his psychic energy on staying out of trouble, and that was a problem. When a child is trying to stay out of trouble, he is not about the business his genius intends: being all that he can be. More on this concept later.

So what the parents did right was getting back to being loving parents and trusting that their son would work out whatever problems he had with his teacher. The teacher finally started making it clear precisely what backup she wanted at home, and that unless they heard otherwise, they should not worry about misbehavior at school—the school would handle it.

If teachers don't do it, parents should take the initiative, form a team, and make crisis-management plans with the other child-rearers in their lives. Think of the constructive and fun conversations parents could have with grandparents, babysitters, and teachers. It's much more fun to have them in advance proactively than reactively in fear and desperation. What if the adults made a list of possible undesirable behaviors on the left-hand side of a page and opposite each one wrote the consequence that all the adults would use? What a sense of solidarity. What consistency. It would give the child a sense that there was order in the world, and this would go a long way to preventing undesirable behavior. Besides, it is hard coming up with good consequences all by yourself.

Kids need boundaries, and they push against boundaries to see what happens. It is not bad behavior. It is what a kid is supposed to do. "Testing" is kids learning what is real. Even adults will touch the newly painted wall to see if WET PAINT really means what it says. If, every time kids push against a fence, the same thing happens, they get the idea; they increase their sense of security and self-confidence. They tend to appreciate, support, and obey the rules. But if fences are all over the place, and in some places there are no fences at all, and sometimes you touch a fence and get zapped with eighty volts and other times nothing happens or the fence falls down, a child will spend a great deal of his time pushing on fences and less time getting down to the business of making something of himself in the world.

# 11.

# We Are All New

c∕∽っ

The sharp ring of what my cell phone calls "Pachelbel" drills its metallic tones into my brain. Even though I am awake at ten to six in the morning, listening to the first bird wake up in the cold August fog, it still takes me forever to realize that the noise is pointed at me. In fact, I seem to know that it is violating the sleep of my roommate at our annual faculty retreat before I realize that I am criminally responsible for it. My shame mounts as I leave the room and turn off the call at the same time.

Who can this be?! When the menu of missed calls says "Brooke," my eldest daughter, the professor in Nashville, I am incredulous and punch a nearly random sequence of keys to discover the truth. Then a beep and the liquid crystal display indicate that I have just received a voice-mail message.

This is what my intelligent, responsible, infinitely thoughtful daughter-teacher-wife-mother has to say: "Dad, it's 5:50 in the morning your time." [*Yes, it is, Brooke.*] "So I am glad I didn't wake you up . . ." [*Well, to be honest, you didn't.*] "I just dropped your granddaughter off at kindergarten for her second day, and I want you to know what an amazing feeling it is. I am sending this person, who finally has no more baby in her, off into the world on her own. I just wanted to mark the moment."

Well, Brooke, of course I forgive you. (Whether my room-mate will forgive me is a different matter.) What am I saying? Forgive you? Of course! The daughter of my daughter is now taking her own walk into the world. School opens for me this week also. Now I am awake to what is really going on. Thank you, Brooke, for reminding me of what the moment is really all about. Dozens of little ones just like my daughter's daughter— only completely different, too—will be entrusted to me in two days.

It is an awe-inspiring responsibility to receive all these new young students into the school building. More than five years of love (feeding, talking, waking up in the middle of the night, nursing back to health, resolving conflict, noting the benchmarks of development) are now being tested as little people are released into the complex social and physical environment we call kin-dergarten to begin the mastery of the world on their own. The feeling, for both parents and children, must be akin to the first test flight of a new spaceship.

It's important that we—teachers and parents alike—remem-ber what the first day of school is really all about. We adults, of course, think it is about the beginning of a child's academic career. But we forget. What was it to us? For most of us, it was the chance to find friends and develop relationships.[11]

These two visions of school need not be in conflict, if we see it the children's way. They want to learn to read and write, of course. Every time I ask incoming first-graders what they are looking forward to in first grade, they say, "Homework!" The difference is that for children, everything they do in school is all lumped together under their favorite thing: learning. Only the adults separate out book learning from all learning and make a special case of it. One of the underlying messages of Lucy Calkin's book *Raising Lifelong Learners* is that the children's view is truer: "The qualities that matter most in science and math, reading and writing—initiative, thoughtfulness, curiosity, resourcefulness, perseverance, and imagination—are best nurtured through the 'everydayness' of our shared lives."[12] I would add the rigors of the classroom, too. Best to nurture them in everything we do at school and at home—both.

A school that teaches academics as if the children are inmates in a social and emotional vacuum is making a huge mistake. It's like trying to make a tower of five thousand pennies by piling one on top of the next. School must also be an education. If one wants that tower not to topple but to keep on growing through life, it will be a

> A school that teaches academics as if the students are in a social and emotional vacuum is making a huge mistake.

pyramid with a broad base, not a narrow tower. For lasting results, learning must be multi-dimensional. Even at the top of our pyramid, the last penny sits on a three-dimensional base of cognitive, emotional, and social meaning.

One year at opening assembly, I asked the students what they noticed that was new that year. Someone said, "We are in a new classroom." Others mentioned new classmates, new trees, new teachers, and new lockers. Teija Corse said, "We are all new."

That answer was so insightful that I jumped up on the sandbox we use as a stage and said, "That's right. We are all new. I am going to make a declaration: I am new. Raise your hand if you are new, too." Most of the hands went up. "This is a school where you get to be yourselves, and if you want to be new, you get to be new: make new art, write something new, learn something new, make new friends. That's what we do here."

In creating the conditions for the optimal leading out of the genius, giving ourselves and others permission and encouragement to be new at the beginning of each day, as well as at the beginning of a school year, is a good first move. Humans naturally build self-images around our genius, and those self-images often determine behavior. How each person's self-image plays into what he or she does will be different for each person: "I am the class clown"; "I am popular"; "I am a great reader"; "I am a bad speller"; "I can't do math"; "I am a loser." Self-image shows up in other kinds of "egospeak." Often we define ourselves as being *not* someone else, as in: "School is stupid" (unlike me); "Frieda is conceited" (unlike me); "My mom is, like, *soooooooo* controlling" (unlike me); "My brother is a total geek" (unlike me). To help children grow maximally, we must help them change and transcend these generalizations. Truly loving includes not labeling.

I have the fantasy that at the beginning of their next seventeen years of schooling, each of these new students will sit down with his or her parents and say, "Okay, you guys: I will learn to read and write and solve problems mathematically and any other way you think is good, if you will recognize that I have my interests, I need my friends, and I need to do stuff in my own way in my own time. Most of all, I need to be trusted. I will even let you tell me stuff, remind me, make me do things, as long as you don't start acting like my education is more important to you than it is to me. You may not realize this, but I really appreciate you telling me what you and the world want; just don't start taking it personally, because it's my life, not yours. You know, you guys, I want to learn even more than you want me to."

Since they are only five-year-olds, and they don't know as much as I do yet, let me say it for them. Come on, parents, let's make a deal.

## 12.

# Getting Our Butterflies to Fly in Formation

"Do you know the difference between an amateur and
a professional?"
"No. What's the difference between an amateur and a
professional?"
"A professional gets his butterflies to fly in formation."

On the first day of kindergarten, *die Kinder* were all over the
playground swinging, climbing, and running. A few sat with
their parents on the edge, and most of the adults were chatting
away merrily, happy to see one another again. Some were making new friends.

However, as I went from knot to knot of parents to join in,
the big theme was "My child was a little nervous this morning."
One parent reported that all summer long, every time the
subject of school came up, her daughter would start jumping
up and down and squealing with delight, but when there were
only two days left to go, she got quiet and talked about how
nervous she was.

Another girl, who actually wanted to say hi to me on return-
ing to school, talked with me for a while about the summer and
then said in a low voice, "I have butterflies in my stomach."

I said, "I know. I am nervous, too. Can you believe it? I have been going to school now for fifty-eight years, and I always get nervous before the first day of school." She looked at me with puzzlement and disbelief and ran off to the climbing structure.

Every first day, some kids cry or in various ways make like they don't want to enter the big building, and some kids just run to be first in line. But don't be fooled by the difference. We are all nervous. Our personalities and our upbringing have trained us each to develop our own special reaction to a new social situation. Me, I'm a run-to-the-front-of-the-line person. I figure the best defense is a good offense, but don't be fooled by the smile on my face. Getting up this morning was a 51 to 49 decision.

Others are trying on slow as a better strategy, and some are still working it out. To maximize our children's potential, we must make it safe for them to discover and develop their own ways. As *die Kinder* get older, their characters get more divergent rather than more similar. Each kindergartner gives me a "high five" in his or her own way: Some like to really give me a whack, some prefer an intimate pat, some hit my hand with their heads, and sometimes I get a dodge. There is more variety as the year goes on. Schools and parents need to support the drive to uniqueness even as they teach the disciplines of being effective in the environment.

Getting the first day of school right can make a big difference. It takes discipline. Perhaps the most useful one to remember is: "Treat them as if they know what they are doing." If we are worried, our child will pick up on that and feel that there is something to worry about: "My mom is pretty amazing, very experienced, very knowledgeable; if she is worried, I am sure I should be worried."

Using our disciplines often requires doing some inner work. Many parents have learned a lot from the painful experience of letting their children go off to school on their own. One parent told me that it required her to get in touch with her own fears of abandonment, which went all the way back to her childhood. She said that she kept repeating to herself, "Self do it, Self do it, Self do it." She also said that "Self do it" was not sufficient all by itself. She also needed to keep in mind: "Do the present right; the future will take care of itself. Let go. Let go. Let go."

Letting our kids make their own decisions is hard when we are afraid. It is hard to set boundaries and stick to them when we ourselves are feeling vulnerable. This was certainly true for Michael's parents, who were genuinely afraid for him on the first day of kindergarten. Michael would not leave their side and cried when they tried to leave. Sure enough, in the half hour when students gathered on the playground before entering the building at 8:30, Michael would cling to his mother or father (whichever was dropping him off). If they started to kiss him goodbye, he would begin to cry and cling. If his mother was dropping him off, he would wail when she tried to leave and sometimes even have to be carried into school by the teacher. (Once in the classroom, he would settle down within five minutes, and by the time I visited the room around 9 AM, he was always working merrily away on his schoolwork.)

> **Letting our kids make their own decisions is hard when we are afraid.**

In my conversations with Michael's parents they could not articulate why they were afraid. They weren't concerned that he was slow-witted or disabled in any way they could specify. They just saw him as young and were worried that he wouldn't be able to handle himself in kindergarten. Despite all our suggestions regarding different separation techniques, nothing was working. It was agreed that Michael's father, Percy, was the best person to drop him off. That made the wailing stop, but Michael still seemed to require his father's presence as he swung on the swing or climbed on the climbing equipment.

At our second formal conference in the first week of October, I suggested to Percy that they arrive at school earlier rather than later and that he go straight to a bench on the edge of the playground and just sit there, rather than following Michael around the playground. "Let the playing be his activity, not yours," I said. "If he asks you to follow him or join him on the swings, just say that you don't feel like it or are tired. You will watch him but not join him. You just want to sit. This will set up a choice for Michael: He can stay with his father and sit on the bench while the other kids are playing, or he can go off and play on his own, but he can't have both. It is a way of defining reality to him: 'I love you, and I have my business, my life; you have yours and it's all OK.'"

Percy tried it the following day. They walked in through the gate hand in hand, but instead of going to the swings, Percy went to the bench and sat down.

"Let's go swing," Michael said.

"No, I don't want to today. I'll just sit here. You go swing."

Michael hesitated before he said, "C'mon, I want to swing. Come with me."

"No, I don't feel like it today," Percy responded. "It's a beautiful morning. I just want to sit here."

"Aw, c'mon."

"No. I don't want to."

Michael sat down next to his father on the bench and was quiet for a while. Then there were a few more Aw-c'mon's and No-I-don't-want-to's; then more quiet. Then, without a word, Michael got up and went for the swings.

Things changed after that. That giant step of individuation known as the first day of school had finally been taken, and the family could relax. It was a breakthrough caused by using the disciplines with finesse. It was also the first step in a long process, during which parents learned more than child. They began to discover their own fears which they had been projecting onto their son. The myth of their Michael's general weakness began to fade; now they could see his true strengths and weaknesses more accurately. The family was getting its butterflies to fly in formation.

The art of maximizing learning for our children always includes a lot of learning about ourselves. We have to learn the disciplines that will facilitate the individuation of our children. We learn to partner up with our children and to play our positions while we let them play theirs. We learn to learn *from* our children, and to listen to our own "teachers within." We allow ourselves to be changed—to be new. Acting out of love, not fear; allying with the enemy; changing perspective; being self-aware without being too self-critical; knowing when to act and when to wait—we learn all of this. We learn courage, persistence, authenticity, integrity, humility, forgiveness, charity, compassion, patience, mindfulness, trust, and, above all, humor. Seeing these "virtues" as disciplines that need practice is more constructive than thinking of them as personality traits, or as reminders of some theoretical good, short of which we always fall.

# III: It's Academic

# 13.

# Engaging Genius

In a kindergarten class, after hearing a reading of the book *Owl Moon*, many of the children became interested in "owling." When do you go owling? Well, at night, of course! Where do you go owling? The teacher, Candy, looked up where owls might live in San Francisco and discovered that a great horned owl lives in Glen Canyon Park. Birding is one of her hobbies, so she sent a general e-mail to the parents, inviting them to go owling in Glen Canyon one Friday night in early March. That night, most of the class showed up.

They walked along the trail, stopping to call the owl every so often. When they reached its end, they gave one last call. Some were sure they heard the owl call back, ever so faintly, from the other side of the park. Their evening ended then, but not without an agreement to try again in April.

They met again in early April, a bit earlier this time, so there would be more light to see by. Candy had heard from a local resident that the owl had taken up residence and had some babies in an abandoned hawk nest down the trail. She sat the kids down at the side of the trail near the nest and read *Owl Moon* at twilight, and just as they finished the story and gave their own "hoot," one of the parents said, in a loud whisper,

"There he is!" and a large owl went swooping past! It was a very magical moment. They saw both mother and father owl, as well as the nest. It was a night to remember.

The walls of the classroom should not be the boundaries of the education. A child's enthusiasm for learning naturally exists both in and out of school. Parents can have a powerful role in maintaining this, mostly by not getting worked up and anxious about their children's academic achievement. These days, mostly from anxiety, parents get overly involved in homework and begin acting as if schoolwork is unnatural, their kids are not going to like it, and they had better do some teaching at home as well if their children are going to measure up. This can be very destructive. Kids need teachers in school and parents at home.

**Kids need teachers in school and parents at home.**

It is natural for children to see the world as full of wonder; why isn't it natural and common for an educational program to be designed so that it engages that wonder and guides it into full-blown, disciplined intellectual curiosity? When it does happen, it is a joy. It also shows up in academic performance, from a second-grader who wants to stay up past her bedtime to do more multiplication to a seventh-grader whose determination to complete some writing she had been struggling with drives her to a moment of brilliance. Often, students' enthusiasm for what they are learning spills over to reawaken that enthusiasm in their parents. Another interesting result is a feeling of generosity that pervades the entire school culture. People give because their hearts are full.

In a national culture driven by aspiration for success (and fear of failure), we need schools to be cultures of inspiration. There is no conflict between inspiration and success; in fact, the former is an essential ingredient. Inspiration is a manifestation of genius engaged. In our fear-driven American culture, educators and parents need to remember and remind one another of the determinants of success. IQ does not predict success. Neither do grades in school, nor scores on standardized tests of achievement. (Research going back two generations consistently shows that the only thing SAT scores predict are grades in freshman year of college.[13]) One thing that does predict success, however, is the passionate pursuit of interests.

Intellectual curiosity need not diminish as students move from playful kindergarten to "serious" middle school, where preparation for high school is critical. When eighth-graders are the product of a culture of inspiration, they impress the high school admission people with their authentic comfort, confidence, competence, and curiosity. Ask any high school teacher what she wants in a student, and she will tell you things like: students who ask good questions, who are not afraid to take risks, who can work well with others, who are good critical thinkers, who love learning. Stands to reason, right? She will rarely say anything about test scores.

Colleges are increasingly focusing on writing as one of the key criteria for admission. They seem to have found a correlation between good writers and success in their programs. But what is good writing, and how do you get it? It is a many-faceted project, but engaging the students' genius is central to the endeavor. There are many components to teaching writing, and writing well is greater than the sum of its parts.

I saw a perfect example of this a few years ago when I taught a class of fourth- and fifth-graders in order to give the teachers some free time to work with one another on the curriculum. One of the students' assignments each week was to learn nine words. They get the words on Monday, look them up, learn the definitions, use them in sentences, and become familiar with them. They came to know these words—in some cases intimately—as they discussed their different meanings in class and the different roles they can play in a sentence.

By Thursday, when I taught the class, they were reading the stories they had written using all nine words. They took turns standing in the center of the room—each one poised and proud—reading their pieces. Then the hands went up. Here were some of their comments:

"I really liked the story. I mean, it was a real story. I would like to learn more about the character. The only word that seemed forced was 'communism.'"

"That was a very nice piece. I want to know what happens. I think you should finish it—I mean not for homework—just, you know, finish it."

"I liked the efficient way you used 'tragedy' and 'catastrophe' right at the beginning by using them dramatically."

"Yes, that was good, but we are supposed to use them so that it is obvious what they mean from the way we use them, and I don't think tone of voice counts."

"It has a good plot; I am interested; I want to know more. But the part about 'rural' and 'urban'—that seemed just stuck in there."

The students were so disciplined that in half an hour we had read and critiqued five stories and one poem. The class almost ran itself. The only thing I "taught" was: "When you use 'but' in giving criticism, it erases the part of your sentence that comes before it. Say it again using 'and.'"

I was impressed by their disciplined approach to literature, even when their own classmates were the authors. I was impressed by the way they were able to give and receive criticism (there was only one moment of slight defensiveness, and

it was quickly corrected). They were so confident and supportive of one another. One of the last comments was from someone
who hadn't had a chance to read:

"This is for everyone. We were supposed to take nine very
hard words..."

"Only seven were really hard," corrected a friend.

"Yes, seven hard ones," he continued, "and force them into
a story. It was really good—well, like, you couldn't tell that you
were doing that. They all sounded like real stories. I couldn't tell
that it was an assignment."

What a remarkable comment to come from an eleven-year-
old! And I agreed with him. It was as if every student had been
able to do two things at once—to use the words they had just put
into their heads, and still to *write from the heart*. Ten-year-olds
have not yet broken themselves down into their component
parts. What their classmates think of them, their values, their
opinions, what they know, how they feel, are all balled into one.

Even though they will be analyzing themselves increasingly
in the course of the next ten years, it is neither necessary nor
desirable for education to become fragmented. Howard Gardner
(a Harvard education professor and the author of *Frames of
Mind*, a book about multiple intelligences) says in his recent
book *The Disciplined Mind* that education involves "motivation,
emotions, social and moral practices and values. Unless these
facets of the person are incorporated into daily practice, education is likely to be ineffective."[14]

One of the important dimensions of education that the "back
to basics" people and the No Child Left Behind project* leave
out as they focus on "basic skills" is the prefrontal cortex. To
function effectively in the world—both in and out of school—a

---

*A public-school-teacher friend of mine calls it "No Child Left Alive."

77

person needs to use his or her prefrontal cortex a lot. This part of the brain deals with complex problem-solving, self-monitoring, and abstract thinking skills. It is required for flexibility of thought and the ability to hold and manipulate information in working memory.

Therefore, assessments of academic achievement must include what some educators have started calling the "executive function." An assessment of the executive function would include:

- Planning
- Initiating action
- Organizing time and materials
- Self-monitoring
- Adjusting behavior to meet the demands of the situation
- Utilizing feedback from others to guide behavior
- Holding and manipulating information in working memory

"Genius" (one of the nine vocabulary words that my fourth- and fifth-graders had to learn) is the word that ties it all together. In a recently published dictionary, the first definition is usually "extraordinary intellectual power," as in: "There are only a few geniuses in the world." However, farther down, as the fifth meaning, is: "the tutelary [I had to look it up] spirit of a person, place, or institution," as in "Her latest work revealed her genius." The first meaning is recent in our language, but the latter one has been around since ancient times and was the first meaning in most English dictionaries until a generation ago. In *The Soul's Code*, James Hillman makes the case persuasively that our development is not sufficiently explained by some combination of nature and nurture.[15] Studying the lives of people throughout history, for instance, there seems to be a third element: Each of us has a divine spark, the unique me that is becoming. It is somewhat ineffable, but that doesn't mean it isn't there.

I have learned that it is not important (or possible) to try to prove or disprove this theory. What raising and educating children has taught me, however, is that assuming that each child has a genius and acting accordingly provides the proper focus for us all to keep our children's growth integrated and to maximize their potential academically, socially, emotionally, physically, and personally.

Education has always been about leading this genius—this tutelary spirit of a person or character—out into the world to function gracefully and effectively within it. It is about making one's unique gifts useful to the world. Effective teachers always instruct with the understanding that the student has a teacher within. However, our meritocratic culture seems to have lost that understanding. In fear and bad habits, we reduce education to bubbles to be filled in on tests, and worry whether our children will test out as "gifted and talented," or as somehow having a "learning difference." We all have learning differences, for heaven's sake.

What I experienced in my class of fourth- and fifth-graders was not just the result of a good lesson and comes from more than good teachers. Getting a group of students to experience themselves as authors results from these students' having spent several years in a school culture that builds on their natural interest in real-world phenomena, that rewards collective success as much as individual success, that calls them to manifest their gifts to the world rather than to "measure up," that calls them not so much to achieve as to learn, and that simply calls them. A good school gives students the opportunities and the disciplines to discover their callings.

This shows up on the yard when students scrutinize the dirt for little creatures, in an art room spilling over with wonderful creations, in classes where students have wonderful ideas, and on field trips when kids ask good questions. It's literally hanging on the walls.[16] Teachers in such a school teach out of love—love of children, to be sure, but also love of interesting things and love of learning.

Getting those test scores to go up will require that the child be enthusiastic about going to school every day, and for this we need to engage the genius. For best results, teachers want their students to be enthusiastic about what they are learning. There is nothing "soft" about enthusiasm. The word comes from the Greek *enthousiasmos*, "imbued with the divine." When the child is enthusiastic, we are at least halfway to success. We want their spirits to be engaged.

Learning is shallow and temporary when a person's "heart isn't in it." The only times I am any good on the tennis court is when I am "playing out of my head" (the language we use for "not guided by the prefrontal cortex"). When a person is lit from within, we know it's working; otherwise the work is "lackluster." An engaged genius is, also, the main bulwark against the pain of failure. People can sustain disappointment after disappointment when they are inspired. We cannot expect sustained academic achievement unless there is enthusiasm.

Enthusiasm, inspiration, integrity, authenticity, spontaneity, humor, grace, greatness, play, and fun—all these are manifestations that the genius is engaged. All these manifestations of an engaged soul are necessary components of helping our children maximize their learning.

We cannot expect students to go off to college with a love of learning if the only currency of success in school is grades and awards for achievement. We cannot expect our children to be inspired if they think their job is to measure up to standards. We cannot expect to be building a sense of integrity if success for a student requires getting through the eye of some needle. We will not be maximizing self-discipline if for thirteen years, school has been about working for extrinsic rewards and staying out of trouble. We will not maximize students' creative potential if the purpose of school is a preparation for something later, like admission to yet another school. We cannot help a child's natural empathy to grow into full-blown compassion if the compassion is not mutual, or if we use our empathy to manipulate them for our own ends. We cannot lecture students on responsibility, grade them on conformity, and expect them to have internalized a sense of responsibility for their work, themselves, their school, and their community.

# 14.

# Freedom to Read

While waiting for my car to be fixed one rainy Saturday, I walked to a local bookstore, A Clean Well-Lighted Place for Books. In my first minute of browsing, Susan Sontag's *Regarding the Pain of Others* leapt off the table into my hands. The appropriateness of my choice did not escape me as I found a chair and began to read. The car mechanic had told me my wait would be long and the bill high. I was looking for a refuge from pain.

Before long I looked up to find a grandmother saying to an intelligent looking six-year-old, "Sit right here and read." The granny then went off to look for books. The girl sat down across the table from me and immediately plunged into her book.

A few minutes later, I heard a woman saying, "Don't fold the pages back like that. See how it creases them?" The girl stopped right away; the shopkeeper moved on. "What nice people," I thought to myself. The girl's nanny with a stroller rolled over and offered the girl another book, which she took happily.

Ten pages later I looked up. The child, who was by then on what looked like her third book, had just said no to the nanny's offer of yet another one. The nanny's face turned angry. "What's wrong with this book?" the nanny asked, pushing the book at the little reader, who pouted and hunkered down into the one she was already reading.

Just as I read, "The weight of words, the shock of photos," the grandmother came by and ingratiatingly tried to insinuate yet another book into the child's field of vision with bended knee and the words, "Now this looks like a really fun one, sweetheart..." She paused. "Doesn't it?" But when her granddaughter hunched her shoulders and moved her face three inches closer to her book, the grandmother sighed a sigh that lifted my coffee receipt off my side of the table, stood up, shrugged her shoulders, and left again.

I looked back to page twenty-five of Sontag's book and read a quotation from the novelist Henry James: "One finds it in the midst of all this as hard to apply one's words as to endure one's thoughts." Then, as I looked up again to ponder what Henry James had meant, my staring eyes met those of my reading partner. I shifted my focus, and we looked at each other. We smiled simultaneously, and this first smile of hers, though warm, was a little shy. Both a bit embarrassed by this serendipitous intimacy, we looked back at our books.

Later, I looked up, contemplating Sontag's idea that "although with luck an untrained child is as likely as an adult to produce a work of art in photography, the same is not so true with language." I hoped that my new friend would look up, too. But instead, the nanny was back. Again, the young girl rejected two books. This time the nanny slammed them on the table and rolled away again, and my little reader read on, not even looking up.

Time passed in silence, and just as I read, "People are often unable to take in the sufferings of those close to them," the nanny returned with a stack of six books. This time the child pulled her body into an angry little ball in the chair across from me and buried her face all the more defensively in her book. If I had been the girl, my anger would have been so intense that I wouldn't have been able to concentrate on my book. But my reading partner's eyes were moving across the page.

"Why, you ungrateful little . . ." the nanny seethed, and I felt the kind of bond that only shared suffering can engender. Still, the object of my sympathy didn't look up. And I never saw her look up again.

The nanny's hostility was palpable as she looked to the grandmother as if to say, "See how hopeless this child is?" The other "responsible adult" looked back with a helpless expression.

In pain, I turned back to my book to read: "Compassion is an unstable emotion. It needs to be translated into action or it withers." I could do nothing. To intervene would have been to interfere; I had to leave A Clean Well-Lighted Place for Books.

In January 1941, in his State of the Union address, Franklin Roosevelt posited four freedoms: freedom of expression, freedom of religion, freedom from want, and freedom from fear. Let's add a fifth: freedom to read. Reading, though harder for some people than others, is something that humans will naturally learn given the opportunity. In our culture, it is an obvious necessity and should be seen as a right rather than a responsibility.

Unfortunately, it is all too often seen as something else. For children today, reading is something you have to do in order to make it in school. It is therefore something that the adults do to children, rather than with and for them. They do this out of fear of failure, fear that the children will not learn to read soon enough. It can become something you do because your parents want you to. It is often something you do to please a teacher. When this happens, the adults get out of position, and if they take it too far, they preempt the child's natural desire to do it for its own sake.

Way back in the '50s when I was a child, my parents read to me. It was wonderful. I still remember some great books: *Katie and the Big Snow, The Little House, Mike Mulligan and His Steam Shovel*. Dr. Seuss was in there with *If I Ran the Zoo* (which is probably why I became a headmaster) and *McElligot's Pool* (which fed my adventurousness). And, of course, *Goodnight Moon*.

Then there was first grade. I remember my first reading group. I remember struggling with "See Jane run. Look, look, look," but that was okay. I thought that was the deal, and I didn't expect it to be a breeze. In fact, I always expect to struggle the first time I do something. Besides, I noticed none of my classmates were whipping through this stuff the way my parents did. Most significantly, Johnny Frankel, with whom I compared myself, was somewhat halting in his approach to words, too.

One day, however, I discovered I was in a different group than the one my buddy Johnny was in, and I asked the teacher why.

"Because that's the fast reading group."

"But Johnny is in that group, and I am as good as him."

"No, you're not," the teacher replied.

I stopped struggling with reading and spent the next four years struggling with the adults who were trying to teach it to me. When I was in fourth grade and had to do book reports, I would pick books like *Paddle to the Sea,* which had great pictures that took up three quarters of the page. I was intimidated by the words.

Then, the summer I was ten, my mother read *The Battle of Britain* to me. Halfway through, she said it was time for her to go start dinner. I protested, but to no avail. She had to start dinner. So there I was, sitting on the couch with a book I was passionate about finishing. So I did. I finished the whole story before dinner.

Our society is nuts about reading because the educational establishment has convinced the public that success in life is dependent upon reading. But reading is something most humans can learn to do, just as they learn how to speak. When we begin to speak, we start out with something as accurate as "Mama." The adult response is not, "No, that is not how you say my name. The correct word is 'Mommy.'" We say, "Oh, she's talking! She's talking!"

It is natural for children, when they are ready, to notice letters and words in the world around them, as they are riding in the car or walking around shopping areas. Letters are as important a part of their environment as are animals—they are more prevalent, actually. In some ways, writing precedes reading. When practicing writing, children get a chance to use an ability they already have (representing something with a crayon or a marker) to learn the letters. Coaching by adults in teachable moments is at least as effective as a reading group—with some kids, more so.

A friend of mine who is the CEO of a Fortune 500 company told me that she thought that early reading was important for the future success of children. "These days, if you are not reading by the time you are in kindergarten, you are going to be behind, and the behinder you are the behinder you get," she said. She was expressing a feeling that, in the thirty years that I have been a school principal, has grown into a powerful anxiety. But the anxiety is misplaced: Fear of falling behind in reading is a manifestation of the increasingly anxiety-ridden, meritocratic society we live in.

Letting this anxiety drive what we do in schools is destructive. Schools pass the anxiety to the parents, and the parents pass it back to the schools in a self-reinforcing spiral that interferes with rather than helps children's ability to read. In fact, early skill mastery does not correlate with success of any sort. Children have different brains and learn at different rates; some very smart people are very slow to develop in certain areas. Pushing books on kids is, as my father used to say, "worse than useless."

Language development is important. Parents should be talking to their children as much as possible as early as possible (right away, in fact, even though they can't talk back). Use as many words as you can. Talking to your child as if she understands not only

> **If parents believe in their children, the children can overcome most obstacles.**

builds strong language pathways in the brain, but also develops self-confidence—and self-confidence should be our focus, not reading. If parents believe in their children, they can overcome most obstacles.

It is the same with reading to children. Reading to them every night before they go to bed is not only an important foundation for their learning to read—for some kids, it is all they need, and they go to school reading. But (duh) it is also fun. For as long as humans have been human, storytelling has been a foundation of education. Reading to children serves many of the same purposes. It is, of course, worth doing for the relationship alone. When you add to that the modeling, the vocabulary development, the insights, the pleasure, and all that can be learned through books, it is a wonder that parents aren't doing it constantly. Read to your children every night, and it will be impossible for them not to learn to read.

To be sure, children need to be taught reading skills, but how reading is taught is critical. Parents should get children to tell their own stories, write and illustrate them, direct and act in plays of their own creation. That is, parents should tap into their children's personal energy as much as possible. Lucy Calkins says, "Children need to be inducted into the tradition of reliving and rethinking moments of their lives. This isn't a minor detail in a child's education; it is essential."[17]

Some children pick up reading as if by osmosis by the age of four. Others find reading a mystery well into third grade. Brains are different, and good teaching includes a variety of different approaches. For example, phonics is necessary for some kids and unnecessary for others. The system needs to be flexible, so that we are always treating the child as if she is already a reader.

Children's interests are not something to be thwarted, but cherished, worked with, and developed. Interest is nature's way of guiding a mammal to those activities that will cause optimal brain development. In humans, interest is also the voice of character—what we find interesting is one of the ways our genius speaks to us. Imposing books on children is not just a bad strategy; it is a violation of their souls.

> Interest is nature's way of guiding the person to those activities that will cause optimal brain development. Interest is the voice of character.

I don't know anything about the three individuals who worked their way into my consciousness at A Clean Well-Lighted Place for Books. I don't know how willful or stubborn the girl is. I don't know her relationship to the two adults. I do not know their history, or which side of the bed any of them got up on that morning. I do know it was not a good idea for the nanny to assault that little girl with books. It was a violation of her genius and a basic human right: her freedom to read.

# 15.

# Acceleration

A grandparent once emailed me:

*I was particularly attentive to the concept of accelerating kids in the last two articles and would like to hear more about acceleration in academics. Part of me knows that it is not good to rush kids through higher and higher levels of achievement, but I am still tempted by the idea that it is good for my grandson to be academically advanced.*

This grandparent is in good company. These days, his second feeling resonates strongly in the hearts of many parents as they consider their children's chances for success. Perhaps this is a case of words causing misunderstandings. Acceleration connects in my brain to the concept of getting ahead of oneself.

In eighth-grader Ethan Haslam's paper, "Impeachment Trial without the Defendant," he concludes:

Why Blagojevich continues to compare himself to great heroes and insist he's done nothing wrong is simply astounding to me. I find it interesting that politics, one of the most important businesses in the world, is more corrupt than almost any other business, especially since politics needs to be the least corrupt. I suppose the power that comes with high office can make people reckless and make them forget that, even if you're the president, bad deeds have repercussions.

Is this advanced? I guess so; Ethan is 14 years old and writes like an adult. Acceleration? No. He arrived at this level of academic proficiency because year after year his teachers presented him with activities which challenged him to mobilize his interests, values, and abilities toward accomplishing something. We've always tried to design things so that Ethan could bring all of Ethan to a situation. The ball we are keeping our eye on is his genius. Ethan's spirit, his character, his calling to make something of himself, whatever his abilities or disabilities may be, must always be our core mission.

This September Ethan will be going to a great high school. Although we do not yet know which one, no one should worry (although I am sure he and his parents are a little anxious). Someone who can write like this can also think well. It also seems fair to infer that his thoughts are connected to his feelings, his values and indeed, his whole self. This is the aim of education. Anything else is mere schooling.

Academic skills are minimum competencies for getting into the next level of education and some of them, like the ability to read and write, are important for success in the civilized world. But minimum means just that. When high schools and colleges spend more time looking at a student's writing than test scores, it is because they can see a whole person in a piece of writing. To get great results, the self must not be left behind. For great academic achievement, we must keep the self at the center, as we challenge students with intellectually rigorous activities.

Educated people are good at handling all of the challenges that college and life throw at them. This is learning all the physical, mental, social, emotional, and spiritual disciplines necessary to harmonize the daily dictates of one's soul with the requirements of the environment. "Top" colleges take mere academic competence as a given. They have more than enough applicants who do well on the SATs. As they look to distinguish one from another, most admission departments don't rank them academically, but look for qualities that might roughly be categorized under the concept of "character."

Therefore, the level of academic achievement of a particular student at a particular time is something to consider in the larger context of the whole child. Getting her to read faster sooner is probably not a good goal. Thinking about and making sense of what she is reading and then writing about it—at her own level of competency—is what will produce the big payoffs later.

One day I happened upon a sixth-grade teacher as he was writing progress reports on students. He stopped what he was doing, looked up, and said, "This girl is a model student. She is exactly what we are looking for in candidates for our school."

I asked, "What's so great?"

"She eagerly tackles any challenge that I give her," he replied.

The work of Carol Dweck at Stanford supports this quality as a criterion with predictive value. In "The Secret to Raising Smart Kids," Dweck reminds us that success is not a function of intelligence measured by a test or a set of fixed gifts or abilities, but a function of applying yourself to the challenges at hand.[18] It is a matter of hard work and disciplines—those behaviors and habits that help us accomplish our goals. Students who believe that they have the ability to grow their intelligence will outperform students who have a notion that intelligence is fixed and who feel that the more of it you have the more successful you will be. Successful people are successful because they work with diligence and discipline to make something of themselves in the world. At the beginning of the article, Dweck writes:

> Our society worships talent, and many people assume that possessing superior intelligence or ability—along with confidence in that ability—is a recipe for success. In fact, however, more than 30 years of scientific investigation suggests that an overemphasis on intellect or talent leaves people vulnerable to failure, fearful of challenges and unwilling to remedy their shortcomings.

The point is critical; inculcating this new notion of the determinants of success into the culture of our homes and schools would revolutionize how we educate children.

It's not their strengths or weaknesses or their level of academic proficiency that makes a difference in the quality of their lives, but their enthusiasm for embracing a challenge and getting down to work. Most admission departments, especially the good ones, agree with this teacher. And yet the pressures of our culture push us to accelerate our kids and act as if the most important thing is ability and current level of achievement.

In "The Crack-Up," F. Scott Fitzgerald defined a "first-rate intelligence" as "the ability to hold two opposed ideas in mind at the same time and still retain the ability to function." In writing about gun control, Miranda, a seventh grader, did a good job of holding two diametrically opposed views together long enough to come up with her own age-appropriate position on the subject:

> It's dangerous for everyone to own guns, but we can't ignore the constitution. And each individual's situation

is different. I think that, under the current constitution, we should have strict gun control with background checks, license requirements and other precautions. But in order not to violate people's rights, people should be able to own guns if they pass certain qualifications and if there are no obvious issues.

One could call this piece of writing academically advanced, I suppose, but we helped Miranda get here not by accelerating her, but by encouraging her always to be on top of her own game.

Many children start to read early and naturally, and it goes hand in hand with writing. One day in early February, Gladys, one of the teachers of the Fireflies, a preschool class of four-year-olds, came into the lounge at lunch time and said: "We have had an outbreak of reading in the Fireflies today."

"Really, that's great," I said. "What do you mean?"

"Well, just that. It was a little epidemic."

"Huh. Wow. What happened?"

"It happens every year right about this time. You know how we always label the kids' work? You know how if they make a picture, we ask them about it, and then we write what they say on a strip of paper and put it under the picture when we hang it on the wall? Or if they create something with blocks and want to save it, we make a sign saying: KAYA, PLEASE SAVE? Well, today, when I was starting to do that for Isabella, she stopped me and said, "No, wait! I want to do it." And she did. She not only wrote "Isabella," but she also copied 'please save' from the sign on another structure. In no time, other kids who were building in the block area saw her do that and wanted to do it, too. They read her sign and then made their own for their buildings. Then Mia, who had just finished a painting, asked for a marker so she could put her name on her painting. It went on like that all day, until about half the kids had at least written their own names."

Reading is a natural act for *Homo sapiens* in a literate culture. Children pick it up like they pick up oral language. It's not that we don't have to teach it; it's that we have to teach it cleverly. It is very unclever to teach it as if we are going have to drill it into them through practice alone. Practice is good, but the practice needs to be in just the right context.

The most unclever thing we can do is to *try* to make reading and writing happen before the mind is ready. We must remember to keep one's eye on the long haul. Many mistakes that adults make with children can be reduced to trying to get "results" too soon. Focusing on learning for life and on maintaining a love of learning is essential for maximizing academic achievement in both the short and long run without incurring the negative side effects that attend trying to get results before results can be gotten. We maximize academic potential when we give ourselves the time.

> **Keep your eye on the long haul. Many mistakes that adults make with children can be reduced to trying to get "results" too soon.**

Once I interviewed an AMI-trained Montessori teacher for one of our teaching positions. She was a good candidate—bright, articulate, and very capable. The conversation drifted to children's "sensitive periods," or optimal times for learning certain things, something all good teachers know. Just as I was about done with the subject, however, she said, "If you miss teaching the right thing at the right time, you miss an important opportunity, and then it's gone forever."

Like so much in the business of education, this is a partial truth. She failed to recognize, however, that we *never* know when that "sensitive period" will come for any particular child. When are middle-school students going to master algebra? In truth, it could happen anywhere between the ages of twelve and eighteen; the exact moment is not based on each child's intelligence but on the timing of each child's own peculiar cognitive development.

Some students are already beginning to read in preschool. Many others are not. The average age at which a child is physiologically ready to read is six and a half, but the range is between three and nine. Some students in most kindergartens are reading words; some are reading sentences for meaning. Others will struggle with reading all the way through eighth grade.

A teacher's job is to create the conditions in which children will read and write when they are ready, and to challenge them appropriately. This is quite different from accelerating them. First, as I've said, there is very little correlation between early skill mastery and later academic achievement, creativity, or any other measure of adult effectiveness. Second, focusing on a narrow range of paper-and-pencil academic skills represents an anemic notion of what high academic achievement is all about. Finally, trying to accelerate kids can have serious, negative side effects.

Seeing children not on some black-and-white continuum from strong to weak but as a rainbow of uniqueness is an important discipline in itself. For one thing, it helps us see a label like "dyslexia" as just a handy name that tells us something interesting about how our brains work, rather than as a diagnosis of a disease that puts us at risk for failure.

Several other disciplines of helping children maximize their learning branch from this one, including:

- Working on telling the truth gracefully, rather than emphasizing the positive and avoiding the negative
- Supporting students in leaning into struggle and learning through mistakes and failure
- Developing the habit of honest self-evaluation, facing and owning brutal facts about yourself
- Developing self-confidence through engaging with reality
- Acting as if you are the variable (and everyone else is the constant)

All these are critical when it comes to creating the context in which children will read. Parents cannot make it happen, but they can read to their children every night. They can have lots of books in the house and let themselves be caught reading from time to time. They can talk to their children a lot and ask kids to tell them their stories. Teachers can do a lot too, of course: Reading specialists can teach phonemic awareness and such; learning specialists can diagnose specific dysfunctions and address some of them. However, only the children can read, and if the rest of us play our positions properly, we won't be able to stop them. All of us creating the right emotional atmosphere, with each of us playing our position and only our position—that is the best we can do.

Each brain knits itself together eventually, each in its own unique way. It's a rare brain than cannot eventually master reading.

# 16.

# Abilities, Disabilities, and Success

If you can meet with Triumph and Disaster
And treat those two imposters both the same . . .
Yours is the Earth and everything that's in it . . .
—Rudyard Kipling, "If"

Here it is critical to make the distinction between the "strengths movement" and what I am advocating in this book. In the first sentence of her new book, *Your Child's Strengths*, Jenifer Fox writes:

> After twenty years of researching, studying, and delivering the message about strengths, I look around and see that we still live in a world that is obsessed with remediating weaknesses. There is no place where this is more disconcerting than in our schools.[19]

I have observed this same phenomenon and agree with Fox's concern but disagree with her analysis. Whereas she is saying that we have been spinning our wheels in education because of a focus on remediating weaknesses, I think it is because we have an obsession with ability altogether—the presence or lack of it. I further hypothesize that the reason that twenty years of working on strengths has not produced the change Fox and others have desired is that the strengths movement is barking up the wrong tree. Believing in one's strengths is just the flip side of worrying about one's weaknesses. Both approaches perpetuate the same ignorance, and I predict that neither will improve the quality of learning for our children.

The current strengths movement is a repackaging of a common theme that has been running through American education for at least the last forty or fifty years. It is just a perpetuation of our cultural bias for "being positive."

This same bias also inadvertently perpetuates the fear of failure due to weakness. True, focusing on strengths is an improvement over the standard fear-based achievement orientation. But trying to revolutionize our schools by focusing on kids' strengths is slightly yet fundamentally off the mark.

When my daughter Lizzie was ten, she decided that she wanted to learn to dive. After a few lessons, she practiced on her own a lot. Over and over she would dive off the dock into the lake, and every time her head reappeared above the water she would say, "What did I do wrong?"

I would tell her: "You bent your knees," or "Your feet came apart," or "You bent your knees again," and so on, for what seemed like a hundred dives. It became hard for me to keep telling her she had made a mistake—each dive had something wrong with it. I wanted to say, "That was terrific!" but I couldn't. I did what I was told, and stuck to the truth.

When I told this story in the faculty lounge one day, some of the teachers looked concerned, and one said, "Hmmmm. Negative self-talk." It is still a common opinion in popular psychology that to talk about what is wrong with you is bad for your self-confidence. The opinion is common but wrong as a generalization—a cultural myth, not a scientific reality. The fact that Lizzie kept asking for accurate feedback reflected ego strength, not low self-esteem. She had an ego that was strong enough to want to know the truth.

Contrary to popular opinion, self-confidence (another name for ego strength) is not built by praise and success, by maximizing the positive and minimizing the negative, nor by finding strengths and ignoring weaknesses. Rather, self-confidence is built, as Carol Dweck's work shows, on believing that one's success is a function of factors over which one has some control (like effort, practice, and discipline) not factors over which one has no control. This is particularly important when it comes to academics. Mathematics students, for instance, who believe that a person's mathematical ability is relatively fixed and doesn't change much over time lose motivation, effort, and achievement when they run into difficulty. Those who believe that mathematical ability is something that can change with learning and practice tend to rise to challenges and increase their mastery and competence as their course progresses.[20] I know a number of older students who are very bright but who *can't* do math problems that less able students can do. The conversation with the teacher always goes according to this pattern:

> Teacher: "I want you to try these three problems here."
> Bright student: "I can't do them. They are stupid."

The ability to face facts is a better predictor of success than focusing on strengths and ignoring weaknesses. Distorting reality for the sake of protecting a person's "self-esteem" is bad pedagogy (but disturbingly common). A disciplined teacher, amateur or professional, keeps working on telling the truth gracefully and avoids thinking about what's "positive" and "negative," for whether something is positive or negative is mostly a matter of one's mental attitude in the first place.[21]

In his 1998 work *Extraordinary Minds*, Howard Gardner says, "We are all deviants from the norm in one or more particulars— in the accidents of our birth, or combination of intelligences, the contours of our personality, the particular circumstances that we undergo at home, in school, on the streets. Some of us have quite stunning deviations." We are characters. What makes the difference in determining success or failure is the extent to which we can identify our unusualness and make it work for us.[22]

A parent of a kindergartner once sent me a speech by John Cleese called "The Importance of Mistakes," which included this passage:

> The very first nursery story that my mother ever read me was called "Gordon the Guided Missile."
>
> When Gordon sets off, it sends out signals to discover if it's on course, and signals come back. "No, you are not on course. So change it, up a bit and slightly to the left." Gordon changes course and then, rational little creature that he is, sends out another signal. The missile goes on and on making mistakes, and on and on correcting its behavior in light of feedback, until it blows up the nasty enemy thing.
>
> As a result of making hundreds of little mistakes that could be corrected immediately, eventually the missile succeeded in avoiding the one mistake that would have really mattered—missing the target.
>
> When Edison first produced the light bulb that worked, he explained that he had made more than two hundred attempted light bulbs before one worked. "And how," a journalist asked, "did you feel about all

those mistakes?" "They weren't mistakes," Edison replied (calmly, I'm told). "Every failure told me something that I was able to incorporate in the next attempt."[23]

Our culture has a built-in notion that self-esteem is a function of success, praise, and staying "positive." But in truth, self-esteem is a function of enthusiastic struggle, an important part of which is making mistakes. The strengths-movement formula for success is to identify strengths, set aside weakness,

**Self-esteem is a function of enthusiastic struggle.**

then decide what to do based on a rational calculation of ability to do it. Thinking back on the thousands of children and adults I have worked with over the years, this is not how people discover and develop strengths, achieve successes, and build self-confidence.

It happens more the opposite way. Some mysterious force or motive says, "Do it," "Go for it," "Give it a try." Self proceeds. Then Self gets engaged, experiences some combination of successes and failures, trials and errors. Those who don't let the setbacks get them down keep on going, learn, and discover strengths they never knew they had. They often overcome their weaknesses. (Some Selves proceed cautiously, dipping the toe in first to test the water, while others just plunge in—but either way, motive precedes calculation of ability.) Motivation comes first, and the discovery of strengths comes second.

Maximizing our children's learning is a function of creating an environment where it is safe to be true, where everyone can be "out of the closet" about anything about themselves, where you don't have to be embarrassed. Even in first grade, Adrienne couldn't hold her head up. At first it seemed she was shy, but after a while it seemed like a better guess was that her self-esteem was just very low. As school progressed, her learning disabilities became more apparent. She had difficulty in most aspects of schooling: reading, spelling, arithmetic, and most especially forming letters.

Throughout the years I knew her, she had one or more specialists working with her outside of school, and by dint of her steadfast courage and grit in school, she continued to make progress academically. By seventh grade, she was still having a great deal of trouble with her handwriting. Though she spoke up in class discussions, often with great insight, she still kept her head down.

One day I saw a glorious Adrienne moment in a class I happened to pop in on. When I walked into the room, the students were seated at six tables, four to a table, and Emily, the teacher, was walking among them talking.

"... 'kenning' is a word for this old Nordic poetic device. So what we are going to do is make kennings and see how creative we can get.

"So what I want you to do is for each group to come up with twenty words—nouns—on two pieces of paper—ten on each. When you are done, everyone in the group put up your hands so that I can see. Then decide which paper you will give to another table.

"Then, you see, each table will have two lists, one of theirs and one from that other group. Then each of you get out a sheet of paper of your own and selecting one noun from one list and one from the other, make your own kenning.

"You can create as many as you want, but pick one that you want to present to the class. Pick one and decide what it means, and when you all have at least one, each of you can come up here to the front and sell your word to the group. Pretend you are a salesperson trying to convince a room of poets that they should use your word. Ready? Go."

When the teacher asked for volunteers to come the blackboard, Adrienne's hand was one of the first up. She went to the blackboard and, in a most laborious hand, wrote her fifteen-letter word. She seemed to chisel the letters onto the blackboard, it was so hard for her, but she pressed forward through her job without hesitation. I could read most of the letters.

When she was done, she turned around and saw that one of her twenty-three classmates was waving his hand at her. She called on him, and he said: "I can't read it."

Undaunted, she smiled her big, broad smile and turned around. She didn't even sigh. Everyone was silent as she erased not just the letters I couldn't read, but the whole word and, agonizingly (for me at least), wrote the word out again. She seemed to go a little faster this time, and this time I could read it all: MOTHERINGENUITY. So could everyone else, apparently, because no hands went up as she turned again to face her peers—still with that big smile on her face.

"What is your word, Adrienne? And what does it mean?" asked the teacher.

"*Motheringenuity,*" said Adrienne. "It means the cleverness of mothers, and you need this word. You can use it when you want to show how a parent solved an impossible problem, you can use it when anyone solves a problem in that clever way mothers sometimes do—like magic—and I think the best thing about it is its versatility. You can use it anywhere under any circumstances, referring to anybody and the way they solved their problem—as long as they did it cleverly." She did this with great gusto and enthusiasm, and for her trouble received applause from the class.

Until that event, I had never known just how bad her dysgraphia was; so what was so dramatic for me was how unself-conscious she was. Under similar circumstances, most students wouldn't have participated, for fear of making a fool of themselves in front of their classmates. The pride in her word and the joy she got out of reciting it and saying what it meant was a delight for all. The applause was quite appropriate. It was like her final exam, except that I am sure that she had been performing such final exams all spring long.

When Adrienne graduated a year later, she moved on to one of the more challenging local high schools. I saw her at a reunion ten years after that. She still held her head down, but it would have been hard to tack the label of "shy" onto her or to attribute to her any kind of low self-esteem when you saw how she beamed at the people she greeted.

The authors of the "strengths movement" might use Adrienne's story as an example of a person building her self-confidence by discovering and developing her strengths—except that it didn't happen that way; that is not even half the story. She discovered strengths as, for seven years, she courageously rose daily to the challenges of the classroom. She discovered her strengths as she simultaneously worked on her weaknesses in and out of class. She discovered her strengths by being in an environment where it was safe to be herself. We want her not to use that silly expression "I'm such an idiot."

I know, from the occasional parent-teacher conference I sat in on, that it was not easy. Her parents always looked concerned when talking with me, but never worried. They conveyed confidence and determination. I know that Adrienne was often discouraged, and that her parents and teachers had to remind her that she was OK and that she would do just fine if she just kept on trying to rise to each challenge as it came along.

For sure, focusing on weaknesses is not a good thing. The more adults focus on them, the more children get concerned about them, and the more they dominate the children's consciousness. But focusing on the opposite keeps reminding us of the very weakness we are trying to ignore, and more important, undermines our motivation to just get down to work. And while it is true that we should encourage students to come from a place of strength, focusing on strengths keeps us in the realm of our love affair with ability.

In this realm of gifts, talents, and disabilities, the word genius is still understood to be "an unusual gift or talent." Using this definition keeps kids focusing on ability rather than on applying themselves, whatever their unique combination of strengths and weaknesses. We want to engage the genius, that spirit, that authorship within, which all of us have; for genius incorporates and transcends our natural abilities and marches us toward our own version of what success will be for us.

Pursuit of genius transcends this dialectic about ability. Genius is not reducible to a set of strengths. It is always a bit mysterious and ineffable. In fact, often a person is called to a pursuit in the face of dramatic weaknesses. Demosthenes, the great Greek orator, had a speech impediment. So did Moses. Moses protested to God that his disability disqualified him from becoming the leader of his people; God would hear none of it. Moses had his calling, and that was that. He'd best get on with it.

It is true that interests often reflect gifts, and gifts that manifest themselves as our genius lead us out into the world, but our genius is greater than the composite of our peculiar set of strengths and drives us to pursue interests for which we never thought we had the ability. Our genius knows we can do it, even if we have our doubts. We must follow it.

# 17.

# Being Literate

The No Child Left Behind Act has accomplished what many educators predicted: It has ensured that those who usually get left behind get left behind. It has done this by requiring some schools—not the best ones—to keep their eyes on the wrong ball, namely standards, rather than on the quality of teaching.

Standards do not ensure good teaching. In fact, standards that are bureaucratically imposed can go a long way to reduce the quality of teaching. One educational fad that has risen to prominence and then fallen again three times in the course of my career is the "teacher-proof curriculum." What an insult to teachers! What kind of person would want to teach if nothing were required of them but to follow the directions of a committee of some market-driven publisher and to keep order among bored students?

Good teachers teach with the assumption that their students can think—not only can think, but must think better in order to be successful. Somehow our society has developed the notion that thinking is all well and good, but first you need to learn your three **R**s. In truth, it is the other way around: To learn the three **R**s, you have to first engage the brain.

In his latest book, *Five Minds for the Future,* Howard Gardner has summarized five sets of capabilities of a well-trained mind, a mind necessary for effective functioning in the world today:

- Expertise in a field (characteristic of the disciplined mind)
- Scanning and weaving into coherence (characteristic of the synthesizing mind )
- Discovery and innovation (characteristic of the creating mind)
- Open-mindedness and inclusiveness (characteristic of the respectful mind)
- Moral courage (characteristic of the ethical mind)[24]

Note that these are "skills," not "gifts," and that anyone can acquire them. The twin approaches that will result in the acquisition of these skills are: **1)** making them the goals of education, and **2)** strengthening the prefrontal cortex of the brain (a process formerly known as hard work and discipline).

The Educational Testing Service (which produces the SAT) has a new Personal Potential Index, a one-to-five scale for analyzing the letters of recommendation that accompany a candidate's GRE scores to graduate school. Its criteria?

- Knowledge and creativity
- Communication skills
- Teamwork
- Resilience, planning, and organization
- Ethics and integrity

The themes are pretty obvious, and the idea that an educated person reveals all of these skill sets is not new. Educators have known for generations—centuries, actually—that education entails all this. What is perhaps new is that America seems to be waking up to the fact that schools need to do more than just grind kids toward fulfilling limited "academic standards."

If one walks into a school that is in pursuit of literacy, rather than just "teaching kids to read," you will see students doing many of the following things:

- Researching topics of interest in books of interest
- Writing in journals
- Sharing stories and creating puppet shows
- Expressing themselves in artistic creations
- Writing descriptions
- Writing directions
- Describing art
- Collecting data and composing hypotheses
- Designing letter writing campaigns
- Reading books to other students—older and younger
- Documenting one another's experiences
- Labeling everything in the room
- Finding the stories behind words and tracking their journey through time
- Writing their personal stories into plays and performing these plays

In one sixth-grade class I am familiar with, the students had little interest in the dictionary until the teacher named it "Huey." Immediately, Huey came into constant use. Magic? Sure. But then great teaching has always been about finding the magic.

Students shouldn't do these things *just* because they are fun, though; they must do them to become educated people. Being literate is more than just rising on the ladder from getting cat out of *c-a-t* to becoming absorbed in Harry Potter's latest adventure. Literacy is a manifestation of the full development of the human organism. Pursuing full development entails everything from playing during recess to making art to solving algebraic equations.

So being literate is not just reading; it is integrating the whole, thoughtful, feeling, imaginative, creative, empathetic person. At the core of this enterprise is the soul of the child and the search for meaning. For best results, we must keep our eye on the full engagement of the students, for only then can we trust that we are maximizing their academic potential.

# IV: Letting Them Struggle

*(Struggle, Failure, Disappointment, Loss, and Suffering Are Opportunities)*

# 18.

# Getting Our Geniuses to Dance Together

On the second day of school, Sofia was sitting on a bench, crying. I sat down next to her and asked her what the matter was. She said, "I want my mommy. I want my daddy." And for a while, this was her response to everything I said.

Then I asked, "What's your mommy's name?"

"Elizabeth."

"What's your daddy's name?"

"Jay." She stopped crying to say it.

"Do you know what my name is?"

"Yes."

"What is it?"

"Mr. Rick."

"That's right! How do you know my name already?"

"My mommy told me."

"Your mommy's name is Elizabeth, right?"

"Yes, and this summer . . ." and she was off, telling me one thing after another without punctuation. Then she said, "I know how to climb. Want to see?"

"Sure," I said. "You show me." And she was off to climb on the play structure, until she was back to tell me that a teacher had told her she had to be in kindergarten before she could climb on the monkey bars.

"Oh, yes, that's right," I said. "You have to wait till you're older to do that."

"Yes. When I am older I can do that."

"Right."

"I can slide down the slide lying down. Want to see?"

"Yes. You show me."

After watching her on the slide, I got talking with a parent. When I saw Sofia next, it was the end of the day. She had had a great day, and I learned three new names, enjoyed a wonderful conversation, and had an idea. To get Sofia from dependence to independence was a simple matter of changing the subject.

Inside each of us is a complicated emotional terrain. We have hills and valleys, with some mountaintops of ecstasy and pits of despair. Most of us—certainly kids on the first days of school—are walking a trail up a mountainside. It's exciting and exhilarating, especially when a change in our lives gives us an opportunity to go to new heights. But higher can also be scary, and sometimes the trail gets narrow, the mountainside steep, and we realize that we might lose our footing and go down instead of up. When we get stuck on a narrow trail, when we're afraid that one more step forward will slide us into the depths, another person can help us find a way forward.

My conversation with Sofia gave me a snapshot of a choice that is with us at each moment of every day: Will I act out of fear or out of love? And as I look back on that conversation, I can see now how close the choice between fear and love is. Sometimes finding that tipping point can be hard, of course, but I was reminded that I had an ally in my effort to move Sofia from fear to love: Sofia herself. Seeing the child as your ally, rather than as a problem to be solved, can help you find the right words to say.

The mind is very creative because the pathways in the brain are myriad. If the familiar path is not working for the organism, the brain gets right to work searching for different routes. In *An Anthropologist on Mars*, Oliver Sacks writes that in the brain,

> there are hundreds of tiny areas crucial for every aspect of perception and behavior (from the perception of color and of motion to, perhaps, the intellectual orientation of the individual). The miracle is how they all cooperate, are integrated together in the creation of a self. . . . I am sometimes moved to wonder whether it may not be necessary to redefine the very concepts of "health" and "disease," to see these in terms of the ability of the organism to create a new organization and order, one that fits its special, altered disposition and needs rather than in the terms of a rigidly defined "norm."[25]

When another person presents us with behavior we don't want (like crying), our natural tendency is to react and when we react feel as if the other person made us behave that way. ("What did you expect me to do? The kid was crying!") It doesn't have to be that way. Sofia presented me with an opportunity to be creative. Certainly I wanted her to stop crying and be happy to be at school, but I let go of what I wanted and just sat with her. Then I thought of something to say: "What's your mommy's name?" Once I had established a conversation, we were both home free. Once I felt freedom of movement, I didn't have to be afraid for Sofia; I could just enjoy her. As soon as I started enjoying her, she cheered right up and went off to play.

Our interactions can be this successful more often than we think. We just have to find a way of giving ourselves freedom of movement. When we feel trapped into a response, the relationship can spiral downward. When we give ourselves the freedom to create a loving interaction, we create the conditions in which the other person can find similar opportunities. We have the infinite complexity of the other person on our side. As Sacks says, even people who are neurologically damaged have a strik- ing ability "to create a new organization and order," one that is adaptive to a changing situation.[26]

An educated person is not simply one who can do well on the SATs. We need to graduate young people whose mental and emotional terrain is networked with a complex of pathways, highways, and byways. This means that as they climb their mountains toward their successes, and a bridge goes out here, or a grizzly bear appears there, they can make choices and can find their way. We all need to work to find the resources within to approach the changing world with courage, to improvise, to act out of love rather than freezing up in fear. This is a good way for each of us to bring our whole selves to the next challenge.

Fear is at the core of the many adult decisions that cause us to get out of position. Out of fear, we fix things that aren't bro- ken, make decisions for our children that are theirs to make, and try to make things easier when challenge is what is called for.

Mark Twain famously said, "I never let my schooling inter- fere with my education." We have to stand together to resist the fear in our culture that is causing school to be only "schooling." Children are naturally inclined to make school an education. The thousands of parents I have worked with actually want this, too, until they get afraid for their children's futures. Teachers certainly know that all the research indicates that maximizing academic potential entails educating the whole child, but educa- tors can also be infected with, be complicit in, or even cause parental anxiety. The future of the human race is dependent on our determined, collective effort to trick ourselves out of being afraid and into making school an education.

# 19.
# Holding Their Hand When They Suffer

~~~

When my son Peter was two years old, we were walking to the school dining room for dinner down a long driveway flanked on both sides by grass and trees. As usual, Peter charged ahead. Running along the side of the road, he suddenly tripped and fell. As he did so, he put his hands out in front of him to catch his fall. When he hit the ground to the right of the asphalt, his right hand struck the broken neck of a bottle that was hidden in the grass. (What were the odds that his hand would land on the only piece of broken glass on a stretch of territory a hundred yards long and thirty feet wide?)

With blood everywhere, we rushed him into town to the emergency room, where he was seen immediately. With me by his side, the doctor and nurse laid him on the operating table to get ready to sew him up. My job was to hold him down tightly so he wouldn't move as the surgeon pushed his needle into the skin and pulled the catgut through the holes.

But even with the painkillers, there was still pain. As Peter screamed, his eyes looked at me beseechingly, begging me to stop it. It required all the work of mind and body for me to keep from giving in to his cries for help and to release him from the pain of being sewn up.

It is so natural, instinctive, and compelling to want to relieve our children from their pain and suffering, but we often must do the unnatural thing. When they struggle and seem to suffer, we need to hold their hands in sympathy but not let them off the hook. It can sometimes be very hard.

When our children go off to school, they are going there not only to laugh and play, but also to suffer. As much learning takes place with tears as with smiles—perhaps more. Brain research shows that people learn more when emotionally involved, but that some emotions can have a negative impact—sometimes emotion can cause the wrong thing to be learned, or the right thing to be overlearned.[27] For the best results, we want emotions that don't have negative side effects, like joy, sorrow, and certain kinds of suffering. (Fear is usually not so good.)

Our children will feel lonely and homesick; they will be anxious before a test; they will complain that something is too hard or that someone is being too hard on them. They will struggle with their homework. They will get into trouble; they will fail or not measure up to their own standards; they will get wrong answers; they will embarrass themselves. The list of possible hardships is endless. Meeting these challenges requires the engagement of the prefrontal cortex, the part of the brain required for making good decisions, setting goals, designing paths to goals, monitoring progress toward goals, delaying gratification, finding order and meaning in the world, and making decisions that help create that order and meaning.

In my experience, American schools and homes are increasingly at risk because they have been trying to engineer children's success. We must let children wrestle with the whole complexity of real life, everything from overstimulation to boredom. We need to be with them when possible to help them sort things out and talk things out, but we shouldn't try to remove the pain.

In the January 17, 2005 edition of *The Washington Post*, Jay Matthews wrote about Zoe Bellars and Brad McGann, two eighth-graders at Swanson Middle School in Arlington, Virginia:

> [They] do their homework faithfully and practice their musical instruments regularly. In a recent delayed-gratification experiment, they declined to accept a dollar bill when told they could wait a week and get two dollars. Those traits might be expected of good students, certainly no big deal. But a study by University of Pennsylvania researchers suggests that self-discipline and self-denial could be a key to saving U.S. schools. According to a recent article by Angela L. Duckworth and Martin E. P. Seligman in the journal *Psychological Science*, self-discipline is a better predictor of academic success than even IQ. "Underachievement among American youth is often blamed on inadequate teachers, boring textbooks, and large class sizes," the researchers said. "We suggest another reason for students falling short of their intellectual potential: their failure to exercise self-discipline.... We believe that many of America's children have trouble making choices that require them to sacrifice short-term pleasure for long-term gain, and that programs that build self-discipline may be the royal road to building academic achievement.

There is no magic wand. It takes thousands of interactions in which disciplines are practiced for us to become good at them. Not to worry: Life provides us with endless opportunities to practice. Raising self-disciplined young people is infinitely complex, and there are many pressures at work in the millions of teachable moments life affords us: "Do your homework"; "Don't talk that way to your little brother"; "Clean up your room."

There is no single right way for parents to handle these things. It is a long-term learning experience for all of us.

We must remember why we are sending our children to school: in the hope that they will be challenged. We subject them to school not for it to be easy for them, but for it to be hard. When they say, "Ouch," we have to resist our natural urge to release them from their pain, just as I had to resist releasing Peter from his. That pain was something he needed to go through, and my being a helper in that experience included steeling myself to ignore his cries for help.

Parenting is a hard job.

# 20.

# Living in the Tension

Character does not grow like a flower; you have to do more than water it. In fact, like grapes for good wine, character develops in adversity. Ralph Waldo Emerson said:

> Difficulties exist to be surmounted. The great heart will no more complain of the obstructions that make success hard, than of the iron walls of the gun which hinder the shot from scattering. It was walled round with iron tube with that purpose, to give it irresistible force in one direction. A strenuous soul hates cheap successes.[28]

Parents play a big role in defining a child's environment. In Emerson's metaphor, the challenges of our environment are like the barrel of a gun; they give our life direction by their very finality. This idea has been all but lost on modern American culture. Our cultural metaphor of the last half-century has been not of iron walls but of hurdles. Opposition is a hurdle to be gotten over, rather than a constraint to be understood and respected. Today the self-respecting, assertive person in the world should blow past or "blow off" the opposition and do exactly what he or she wants to do on the way to the inalienable right of happiness.

But Emerson saw the pursuit of happiness as existing in the tension between an irresistible force of self and the immovable object of its environment. Out of this conflict grows something new, something stronger, something often better than the self had in mind in the first place. The development of character is not simply doing the right thing (the dominant notion of the '50s), nor is it doing your own thing and being "a character." Rather, character (the self-that-is-becoming) is the result of a dynamic relationship between the self and its environment, a tension that educates both the self and others, a conflict that creates new and often wonderful moments—moments of beauty, truth, love, and justice that have never before existed in the world.

In Kansas City in the mid-1970s, Jay was an early reader, and it was obvious to his teachers that he was a brilliant student. His parents were delighted but not surprised. By third grade, however, Jay's teachers were reporting that he was spending all of his free time by himself in a corner, reading. A parent-teacher conference resulted in the consensus that Jay was using reading to avoid social interactions. Even at home, he didn't invite others over to do what most of the kids in Kansas City neighborhoods did back then—i.e., go out and play. Since the main neighborhood pastime at that time was riding bicycles, that was a skill of high social importance. But after school, Jay read. On Saturdays, Jay read. Guess what he did on Sunday before and after church?

One Saturday morning at breakfast, Jay's mom, Marta, said, "Today you are going to ride a bike."

"What? No! I don't want to ride a bike," Jay replied.

"Yes, you do."

"No, I don't. Why do I have to?"

"Because nine-year-olds ride bikes, just like sixteen-year-olds drive cars."

"No, they don't. Not everyone does."

"Name one kid who doesn't," Marta challenged.

"I don't."

"Well, that's just my point. Today you are going to learn to ride a bike."

"I'm not. You can't make me. "

"Don't worry; I will do it with you."

"But I don't want to. I can't."

"Yes, you can."

"No, I can't."

Then Marta said the words that she believes were critical: "You can do it, and I will do it with you."

All day long they rode up and down the street. There was falling. There were tears. But at the end of the day, as the sun went down, Jay was riding his bike. *I'm in this with you, and it's important to me.* Now after school, he rode his bike around and around the neighborhood, right along with all the other kids. His social involvement increased dramatically. He played with the other kids at recess. Even though he continued to love reading, he didn't do it all the time anymore.

Three lessons:

1. Supporting the genius is not about parents backing off. It may require increased involvement. What makes the difference is the quality of the involvement. Devoting a Saturday to bike riding represents more involvement, not less.

2. Supporting genius does not require allowing the child to choose all the time—although allowing choice is often very important.

3. We adults often don't so much need to make stuff happen ourselves as to *be with* the child as the child tries to make stuff happen.

It is also important to remember that kids don't like it when things are too easy. Character needs challenge. We often think

**Kids don't like it when things are too easy.**

we are doing them a favor when we make things easier for them, but actually it can be demoralizing: "What? You don't think I can handle more than that?" Both parents and teachers would really rather a child came home saying, "I don't understand the homework," than saying, "The work we are getting is way too easy; I've had it all before."

When Peter was five years old, I taught him how to ice-skate. As soon as we had our skates on and were on the verge of the frozen pond, I said, "Here's how it goes." I took three steps onto the ice and fell. Looking back at him with a big smile on my face, I said, "Come on. You try."

He took five steps and fell, laughing. That's how he got started.

Seeing our children through struggle, disappointment, and failure is at least as important as witnessing their successes and triumphs. To be prepared for life, we all need to practice falling.

# 21.
# What Comes Then Goes

Once upon a time there was a preschooler named Suzy who had a hard time dealing with disappointment. During the day, when she was disappointed, she would break down in tears and say things like, "I will never feel better," and, "My friends will never be my friends again."

Suzy found disappointment in many things: if her "best friend" didn't sit next to her during group time or lunch; if her friends chose games to play that she didn't want to play; if a friend could do something like ride a tricycle before she could; if she didn't get a turn to speak at meeting time. In all such cases, she would become disconsolate.

The teachers tried everything they could think of: giving her comforting advice, redirecting her, distracting her. Yet nothing worked. The teachers found a bench for her to go to when she was having these intense feelings, but that didn't seem to help either.

One day out in the yard, Suzy was again hemmed in by disappointment on all sides. The teacher asked, "What can you do to help yourself feel better?"

She paused and then said, "I just don't know." The teacher was quiet and just looked at her closely, saying nothing. Suzy said, "I can think of some words to say to myself; then I'll feel better." She stopped crying, but was quiet for a while.

"What are those words?" the teacher asked, waiting for her.

"What comes then goes," the girl said.

"What comes then goes," the teacher repeated. "That is so beautiful. Tell me what you mean."

"I mean when there's disappointment, like I don't like what is happening or what someone is doing, it comes, then it just goes." The teacher saw Suzy's face and body relax, as if all the disappointment had been lifted. Ever since then, Suzy has been moving through her preschool days, on through kindergarten, then on to first grade in full swing. It still seems that she has mastered the art of handling her disappointments gracefully.

"What comes then goes." It's a discipline that Suzy discovered on her own. However, the teacher led her to it. Her opening question was important: "What can you do to make yourself feel better?" shifted the responsibility from the adult (who of course was responsible for Suzy's welfare and passionately wanted to make a change in her) to the child. Suzy was in the habit of letting the adults take responsibility for her problems. The teacher's question changed the paradigm in the child's mind. The teacher recognized the importance of letting the child wrestle with her discomfort, for she knew that the discomfort could provide the impetus for learning.

The next-most-important move was waiting. Once the responsibility had been subtly shifted, it was time to wait for the child to fill the responsibility vacuum. And she did.

In calling Suzy's idea "beautiful," the teacher picked just the right word. *Beautiful, great, awesome,* and *amazing* all resonate in the soul. Words like *good, excellent,* and *right* go to parts of the brain having to do with evaluation and morality; this is not what we are after. We want the child to feel her own inspiration without judgment.

Finally, the teacher helped Suzy build on her idea by asking her to say more. When a child's insight adds to the world, it is worth noticing, building on, and treasuring. Because it's true: "What comes then goes."

# 22.

# Enthusiastic Struggle

One Monday in October, Sonja's mother was in my office, complaining about our writing program. She was wondering if we were ever going to teach grammar and writing mechanics. My response—"Yes, and we already are"—didn't do any good. She complained about Sonja's low test scores in writing mechanics and also about her fear of writing: "At night she is frozen in fear and frustration over writing assignments. She can't get the words to flow." I know it must have been very painful at home; it was painful even for me to hear that every time Sonja had an assignment, she would cry at the keyboard. She would sometimes agonize over it until midnight.

My efforts to help Sonja's mother see that her daughter was going through exactly what she needed to go through, and that supporting her included a mother's calm confidence in her daughter, seemed to fall on deaf ears. So imagine my delight when Sonja herself produced this wonderful story about struggle three days later.

**Over Rated** *By Sonja Carlson*
Many of my friends say that the zip line was the best part of the ropes course, I hated it. It's not what it's

cracked up to be, it's scary, and one wrong move from your belay team, and you could be a goner. Of course, then there's that ever so frightening look down. Being 50 feet in the air and looking down is not the smartest idea. If all of that isn't bad enough, jumping off that high ledge is the worst. When you first jump, you fall down about 10 feet, and then you zoom forward at what feels like 15 mph for about 100 feet. When my group leader asked us to decide the order that people would go on the zip, everyone wanted to be first. I wanted to be last. I wanted to have time to think about if I was really going to go. I kept changing my mind, eventually I just wanted to ask my team members if anyone wanted to switch with me. I just wanted to get it over with. I didn't ask, though; I waited for my turn to come. After waiting for an extremely long time, my turn came. After having my harness checked, I stood and looked at the ladder, and up at the person above me. That was when I told myself that I was going to do this. I put my foot on the ladder and started to climb.

After a few minutes of climbing I reached for the top ledge. I stood up and made the mistake of looking down. I immediately turned away. I wasn't going to let fear stop me. Then I heard "You're clipped in," and I stepped to the edge. I waited a few seconds for my head to stop spinning. Then I jumped off the ledge. I screamed my brains out, and squozed my eyes so tightly that I could see stars. I opened my eyes, and I felt like I was flying. Mr. Rob came over and grabbed my foot and pulled me over to a ladder. I unhooked myself, and stepped down. I thought that I would feel great, because I had completed something that everyone thought was fabulous. I was disappointed though, I felt empty, unsuccessful. I didn't feel any different from when I had started. I had worried so much about something that felt like nothing.

In one clever stroke, Sonja showed us that she was a good writer and that her mother's fears were unfounded, gave us a fine little window into what the struggle of facing up to your fears looks and feels like from the inside of an eleven-year-old, created a new word ("squoze"), got some material for her college essays, and gave us a nice snapshot of genius in action.

## Afterword

When I wrote about this episode in Sonja's life in the school newsletter, I carelessly spelled her name "Sonia." I found a note on my desk the next day that read:

*Dear Mr. Rjck,*
*I liked the story you wrote this week, but I have to tell you that you spelled my name wrong. I did like the story though.*
*Yours truly, Sonja*

## Epilogue

Five years later, Sonja's mother sent me the following email:

*Rjck,*
*John and I just returned from parent-teacher conferences (you know Sonja is a junior now) and again received glowing reviews. Sonja is a bit of a big nut this year: AP Chem, honors Spanish IV (!), honors History, Pre-Calc, and a fabulous honors English course titled "Literature and Ethics." To my delight, she tested out of "Writing for College." Remember me as the parent in tears about her writing ability?*

*What is most satisfying is not her stellar academic performance but comments like "thoughtful," "considerate," "inclusive."*

*Thanks for everything, Susie*

# 23.
# Which Way Success?

After his freshman year in college, Peter Ackerly dropped out. During that summer he lived with me, his stepmother, and his two half-sisters in Oakland and worked at my school, helping the site manager get the school ready for the next academic year. Having him around made it a great summer for me, but a very painful one for him. We had many long talks.

All summer, the tangle of thoughts and feelings that had been spinning around in his head the previous school year came blurting out of him one conversation at a time, as if he were having a hard time vomiting. Each conversation had a point, which he approached cautiously, often beginning the conversation with some obtuse thought and progressively getting more pointed until he finally came out with it. The first one was, "I want to drop out of college for a year or at least a semester."

The next one began, "I really like James [the janitor he was working with as a summer job]. He is brilliant. It really scares me."

"What scares you?" I asked.

"In so many ways, he is just like me." Later that afternoon, over a cup of coffee, he added, "I am terrified I will end up like him."

Then it came out that he had been living with a woman in Appleton, Wisconsin.

Then came the story about the Mackenzie Learning Center. One day that spring, he had been feeling so demoralized as a student that he stopped into the local establishment in Appleton that dealt with learning disabilities to talk to someone. He was desperate to figure out what was wrong with him; he read so slowly and studied so poorly. "Everybody keeps telling me I am brilliant, but I don't feel it," he said. He was told that he had either an attention-deficit disorder or dyslexia.

Then, in the kitchen, when he was having trouble finding the tea bags, he said, "I am not a space cadet!"

Another day he said, "I am reluctantly coming to the conclusion that I am only a C+ student." The music-composition teacher had given him a C+ and told him he would never be a composer. He had gone to Lawrence University because it had a music conservatory. He was not just an oboe player; he felt he was going to be the next Leonard Bernstein. Then he had seen other students more gifted than he, or so he felt. When this teacher gave him this opinion, his self-confidence burst like a soap bubble.

One week later, I heard his frustration that he had been "born into a family of frighteningly high achievers"—not just high achievers, but people "so competitive that they only respect achievement"—and, most important, that he was pretty sure he couldn't measure up.

Somehow I was able to resist my natural propensity to jump in and try to rescue this person I love so much (and identify with). I resisted trying to solve the problem that was causing him so much pain. I don't know why I did not fall into this trap in these conversations with Peter. Perhaps I recognized that this was very serious business—so serious that I had better not mess up; I needed all my professional skill. Perhaps this was because, ironically, his "issues" were so close to my own that I was aware of my powerlessness to solve them and had to resort to letting him talk and listening. In any case, I seemed to have done the right thing. Not trying to solve his problem increased his courage to continue the vomiting process with me.

Finally, on the first of August, it came out that he wanted to go to Helena, Montana, to live with his girlfriend and work as a waiter. Another brilliant move on my part was just saying yes.

On August 4th, my wife and daughters and I drove Peter to the bus stop in downtown Oakland. It was good for him that we adore him so much that we all wanted to see him off, because without all of us, he would have needed to hire some Sherpas to get his stuff from the house to the car and from the car to the bus. His *impedimenta* included one large backpack, one small backpack, one briefcase, one small suitcase, two large suitcases, one box big enough for a kitchen chair, one box that was as big as the kitchen table, and one box that looked big enough to hold a bicycle (and did). All were secured with what must have been an entire roll of tape, plus plenty of string. It looked like he was definitely going to stay.

On October 4th, after two months of silence, I got a phone call.

"Hi, Dad." It was Peter.

"Hi! Where are you?"

"I am in eastern Idaho."

"Eastern Idaho. Wow. Amazing! What are you doing?"

"I am on my bike and on my way to Seattle. I was planning to get on a freighter and work my way over to China. Well, that's what I was going to do, but someone stole my sleeping bag and my tent. What should I do?"

"Wow. That's amazing. Well, how far are you from a Western Union office? I will wire you some money, and you can buy new ones."

"Okay, but is that what you think I should do?"

"Yes. How far are you from a town?"

He told me. "I guess I will go back to the one I just passed."

"Okay," I said. "Call me when you know something."

He called some time later to tell me that the highway patrol had picked up his stuff, that he had it back, and that he was on his way again.

The next phone call, a week later, was from eastern Oregon. "I have changed my mind. How would it be if I came to Oakland instead of Seattle?"

"That would be great! It sure would make me happy," I said. "Is that what you want to do?"

On October 21st he rolled into town, carrying all that he owned in the world on his back and his bicycle. In case you missed it, Peter rode his bicycle more than 1,200 miles across the Rocky Mountains. He arrived back in Oakland with pride in his chest and a song in his head he had composed as he rode, and without all that other baggage he had taken to Helena, Montana, nearly three months ago.

A friend of mine, a professional learning-skills specialist, gave him a series of tests and determined that he would benefit from some intensive training in organizational skills. (He had been tested for "learning disabilities" twice in grade school, but they "couldn't find anything.") Every day for six weeks, he rode his bicycle to the Bay Area Learning Center. By December, he said he was ready to go back to college. He enrolled in the University of Vermont, and at Christmastime moved to his own apartment in Burlington. His grades for the next semester were a B-, a B, an A-, and an A in English.

Of course, the story is not over. People don't "live happily ever after." As of this writing, he is thirty-seven years old, teaching English to Japanese businessmen and businesswomen outside Tokyo, and working on his third novel (none published yet). He has a son, Elijah, whose mother is Japanese.

Conventionally, parents would not worry if their son had, by the age of thirty, settled down, landed a high-paying job, discovered a profession, found a woman and married her, and begun to raise a family. On the other hand, those who already have adult children might well be happy enough if their children have managed to stay away from drugs, AIDS, and jail (all of which Peter has so far been successful in doing), and, most of all, are not living at home.

What is success? How do you know if your child is going to become "a success"? We can't know. There are, however, some indicators we might want to keep our eyes on. Grades in school? No. The research says that there is no correlation between them and measures of adult effectiveness.[29] Test scores? Again, no correlation. Is it the college or high school or preschool your child gets into? No.

The ability to persevere through difficulty? Yes. For as Ernest Hemingway said, "The world breaks everyone and afterward many are strong in the broken places."[30]

Our children are on their own journey. We don't know where they are going. They don't know where they are going. How could we? Though it is almost irresistible to second-guess the path a child takes or suggest different definitions of success, the urge must be resisted. Our children need us to have confidence in them. If we lose confidence, it is our fears that are showing, not their weaknesses. We have no choice but to treat them as if they know what they are doing.

# V: "Normal," Difference, and the Pursuit of Genius

# 24.

# Real Men Wear Pink

John Hooker, a kindergarten teacher, came to class in a pink shirt one day. In kindergarten, there had been a few occasions when students had remarked that a certain toy or activity was "just for boys" or "just for girls." John and his partner, Jen Weiss, were coming in prepared to do some lessons on gender equity. When the students entered class, one of the boys asked with hesitation, "Is that a pink shirt?"

"Yes, why?" John responded.

"Really?" he asked, starting to smirk and cringe his face.

"Yes, pink."

Just before the giggling could ensue, another kindergartner spoke up: "Only a real man can wear pink." This, of course, is exactly what the teachers had been hoping for, and exactly what they needed to start the class off on a day of discussions about biases, stereotypes, and justice.

In the musical comedy *South Pacific*, Lieutenant Cable expresses his rage at racism in a sarcastic song, "You've Got to Be Carefully Taught":

*You've got to be taught to be afraid*
*Of people whose eyes are oddly made*

*And people whose skin is a different shade*
*You've got to be carefully taught*

*You've got to be taught*
*Before it's too late*
*Before you are six*
*Or seven or eight*
*To hate all the people your relatives hate*
*You've got to be carefully taught*[31]

We can relate to the sentiment, but my years in education have taught me that Hammerstein got it backwards. Kids do not have to be carefully taught in order for them to pick up the prejudices of their relatives—that happens naturally. On the contrary, they have to be carefully taught to break down the generalizations they inherit from their culture. They have to be carefully liberated into rigorous and creative thinking.

> **Kids do not have to be carefully taught in order for them to pick up the prejudices of their relatives— that happens naturally.**

All kindergartners can observe in their environment that it is the female who usually wears pink and that the boys tend to be the ones shooting baskets. The idea of a "real man" is more complex than the color of one's shirt. Today, gender complexity is becoming more obvious to us, broadening our notions of what constitutes a real man or woman. A student who can see a pink shirt on a man and turn an old aphorism on its head is a student who will be a good problem-solver in an increasingly complex world.

Teaching about gender equity or social justice is much more than teaching good values like respect and kindness. If our business is to graduate critical thinkers and creative problem-solvers, we need to create an environment in which it is not only safe for a person to express one's gender in any way one wants, but also safe to have new and unusual ideas.

When interviewing teachers, I always ask what they are looking for in a school. In the hundreds of teacher interviews I have had in thirty-some years, most (but not all) candidates are looking for a school in which intellectual challenge is an integral part of academic achievement. They are looking for a school in which teaching is a creative activity. These teachers often report that in so many classrooms (private as well as public), teaching is focusing the students on getting the right answers rather than thinking.

Recently one teacher reported on a school in which, by fifth grade, students were afraid to think creatively about how to solve problems, because the price of getting the wrong answer was too high. By the time he got them in eighth-grade algebra, they were no good at creative problem-solving. In his school, moreover, cheating was the smart way to be successful, since it was the surest way of getting a good grade. Creative thinking in such an environment is too risky.

A long and happy life requires that a person discover his unique being and his unique calling. For this, we need to create the conditions in which each of us can transcend the generalizations we have a tendency to make about ourselves. We need to keep popping one another's stereotypes the way the kindergartners pop soap bubbles on the playground.

There is an intimate connection between teaching students not to be prejudicial of others, helping them to ask good questions and think creatively and getting them not to cheat. These and all other important educational objectives grow out of the quality of the environment parents and teachers create—the quality of the village that is raising the child. Children grow best when they are raised in a culture where all they need to be is all they most fundamentally want to be: socially adept, fearless learners who are comfortable in their own skin. When John wore a pink shirt, he expressed this culture, integrating social justice issues into the day's academic focus with the main point—it is always safe around here to be your own weird self. You don't have to measure up; you don't have to be good; you don't have to conform. You only have to focus on harmonizing your own unique genius with the requirements of the environment.

Education is leading a person out—out of narrow-mindedness and into open fields of possibility, out of banal (and cruel, and false, and stupid) generalities and into an infinite world of unique people and unique events, out of groupthink and into thinking critically for oneself. Education should give us the habits of mind to make each decision in the moment as it comes, on its own merits.

Of course, it is mean to mock someone for the shirt they wear or to make any kind of gender-related slur. In this regard, most kindergartners just need to be reminded about kindness. However, for children's time in school to be an education, we must also create an environment in which these young humans can create something beautiful, something brilliant, some new line of poetry, like, "Only a real man can wear pink."

# 25.

# What's "Normal"?

It is common for a child (for all of us, actually) to feel the pressure of the group and to change behavior accordingly. This is the natural dynamic behind group inclusion and exclusion—peer pressure. It is a necessary part of being human that serves a useful function: A group of people has to become an organism in itself, so the components of this organism (people) have to have some common norms, values, habits, etc. It is important that each of us feel this pressure, or we will be alone, but it also has the downside of inhibiting constructive contributions of the less common.

At the same time, it is also natural for a person to individuate. One of the strengths, in fact, of American culture is its tendency to value the contributions of the unusual. All of us (none more than schoolkids) live in the tension between what we most want to be and what the group seems to want or need us to be. It is, more or less, a healthy tension. Nonetheless, especially in schools, the pressure for conformity can be powerfully inhibiting.

It is also important to remember that what is normal for one group is peculiar for another. Group identity and norms are the result of a unique set of factors, one of which is leadership. If there is a warlike feel to your son's class, it is almost certain that the class has at least one dominant male whose warlike tendencies are dominant in him and who is also a leader.

At one school where I worked, one class was rife with social disturbance. By seventh grade, it had gotten so bad that I found myself talking with students in my office because they had been mean to their classmates or disrespectful of the teachers. The critical point in one such conversation went something like this:

> Principal: "But Gardy, others in the class look to you as
> a leader. Is this the kind of leader you want to be?"
> Gardy: "But that's just it. I don't want to be the leader."

Gardy was the top jock in the class and was therefore the leader, because soccer dominated the social dynamics. When the kindergarten class had formed eight years earlier, Gardy's mother and some other parents had decided to form a soccer team composed only of the members of the class. All were invited to join, of course, boys and girls both, and the team joined the local soccer league. One unintended consequence was that soccer and its norms became too powerful a factor in group identity, causing social standing to be based on a narrow range of values (athleticism). It made some unathletic kids feel bad about themselves and gave others, like Gardy, roles to play that were not right for them.

To maximize academic learning, as well as to promote good social and emotional development and to create the conditions that bring out the best in the students, there needs to be a pluralistic social context, a place where it is safe for each student to be him- or herself. What's normal in a group tends to be taken for granted, but it doesn't have to be. Parents and teachers can collaborate and intentionally design a social environment that is best for everyone, and it can be fun doing it.

But although good teachers always try to create such environments, sometimes they don't have the power to change everything that needs to. Parent leaders can be very helpful. If they see what is happening, they can form a partnership with the teachers and make a plan to change things. The problems in Gardy's class never fully worked themselves out; the kids just grew up, and the class graduated, dispersing to other schools, with each person getting a fresh start. Luckily, some group cultures do not last forever.

### Jorge

Jorge arrived at school from the four-day sixth-grade camping trip dressed like a girl. He had on a skirt and a blouse he had borrowed from one of his classmates, and he had a scarf covering his hair. When I or anyone else greeted him on his return, he said, "I'm Ellen."

Most of the teachers and students who received this news greeted it with a response similar to mine: "Hi, Ellen." I accompanied mine with a bit of a smile, but I know of no one who made a big deal out of this potentially shocking news. The next day, and for the next two weeks, Ellen came to school dressed like a girl and stuck to the story that she was a girl.

Then, as suddenly as she had appeared, Ellen was gone. About three weeks after the trip, Jorge was Jorge again, and business went on as before. To my knowledge, nobody reacted much to the return of Jorge, either.

Years later, I saw Jorge's mother in the supermarket. I told her this story—my side of the story, that is—and finished with the question, "Remember that?"

"Remember?" she said. "Are you kidding? I was terrified."

"I never knew you were terrified. You should have come to talk to me."

"No. It was good. I remembered something you had said at one of our parent meetings about 'underreacting,' and giving kids latitude to discover themselves, and I decided to wait and see. Sure enough, everything turned out just fine. One of the things I learned from the whole experience is that everything would have been fine whichever way Jorge wanted to go. He's a great guy, and we've always known that, and nothing can change that."

"Well, then, double congratulations."

"Guess what else."

"What else?"

"Jorge is going off to Oberlin this fall."

"Well, that's wonderful. Tell him I said hi and congratulations to him."

Helping a child be the person that he or she is becoming is largely a function of making sure the social environment (school and home, primarily) seeks out and values the uniqueness of each individual above all other values. The first question in children's minds on entering a new situation is "Will anyone like me?" Soon, "Will I measure up?" is added, and then, "Am I okay being my own unique, weird self?"

They want to know if those little things they are aware of in themselves will cause them problems in their new environment. And there are so many things children can be worried about: race, socio-economic status, looks, size, shape, athleticism, intelligence, and what they have already learned about their academic abilities. My vision of perfection in a school community is that everyone is "out of the closet" about everything. Kids should be able to say, "I have trouble reading sometimes," or "Running is hard for me," or "It usually takes me a while to warm up."

**"Can I measure up?"**

Self-acceptance is critical, and for self-acceptance the child needs acceptance from others. In truth, most of us can succeed with the hand we have been dealt. The only real inhibitors of success are inhibitors of the genius.

Identifying these inhibitors is not an easy matter, of course. How do we determine which undesirable traits or behaviors need to be addressed, which can be ignored because they will go away, and which are there to educate us?

So much of life is like surfing or skateboarding; it is a matter of balance. Becoming a man or becoming your genius is by no means an exception. I seem to be a mixture of anger and love all the time. As I point myself in a certain direction, I am in love with where I am going. I am joyful when things break my way and angry when I trip myself up or run afoul of something or someone else. Even elementary particles are not static; they are oscillating bits of energy holding steady by vibrating between on and off. I would like to be in love and joyful all the time, but the hell of it is that I find myself vibrating between on and off all day long. So we adults have the job not so much of making our kids turn out "normal," but of helping them become themselves—to be Self the way Self wants to be each day.

# 26.

# Greatness

On a recent visit to a neighboring school, everywhere I looked I saw greatness. I noticed sixth-graders taking notes as they sat in straight rows, listening to a teacher talk about what it was like in Canada when she was in seventh grade; fifth-graders practicing their performance for an assembly; the entire first grade sitting in rapt confidence, collectively working out a complicated pattern; second-graders sorting and graphing an astounding array of tiny objects; third-graders using Venn diagrams to compare the characteristics of realistic and mythical characters; the fourth grade sitting in a circle on the rug talking about cancer; and seventh-graders guessing the correct number from a set of propositions and justifying their choices to their classmates based on those propositions.

Out in the preschool yard, half the little ones were dancing—well, it looked like dancing, but it was physical education. Two grown men—a sixty-year-old and a twenty-five-year-old—were cavorting with sylvan elves who had come out of their hiding places in the woods. That's what it was; there is no other description for it. To say the preschoolers were having PE class would distort reality.

A young woman—presumably the music teacher—was teaching preschool students how to pull stars from the sky and put them in their pockets, and an art teacher was getting some very little people to experiment with color and with different ways to apply paint (with brushes, hands, fingers).

It was hard to see without shouting for joy. Clarity in the eyes, the comfortable bearing of bodies, ease of movement, and always individuality and uniqueness: This was the face of greatness. The relationship between the students and the teachers was one of mutual caring, respect, appreciation, and responsibility—love, actually. The work: engaging, interesting, intellectually challenging. The quality of the interactions between the students: I'm cool—so are you; self-possessed and other-aware; moving through the world with abandon, yet fully conscious. And I saw it wherever I went, even where I saw kids struggling with things that were difficult for them, and even when I knew how hard a teacher was struggling with a particular student.

Greatness. It's a different thing from excellence and the "best." In fact, it's partly the result of liberation from all comparison, for greatness can never be achieved when comparison is involved. If you look over your shoulder to see if there is a person gaining on you, someone will. Fear will kick in, you will become more

> **Greatness can never be achieved when comparison is involved.**

self-conscious, and the greatness that you are will fade—and with it, the quality of your work.

Greatness is the face of the genius engaged. When each character is moving in world gracefully, this is education!

# 27.

# The Sound of Silence

∽

At the Earth Day assembly, three-year-old William Chung raised his hand to make an announcement. Christian Hipolito, the seventh-grade emcee, called on him. William stood up and left his seventh-grade buddy, Duane. He walked to the sandbox (our stage), climbed up on it, and stood looking out at the faces of students, parents, teachers, and administrators of his 250-student school.

But William, who at that moment seemed like the littlest preschooler, did not speak; he just smiled and stood there. Christian, who was standing by his side, didn't move. He offered a word of encouragement, but William said nothing. Christian waited. He leaned over and said, "Whisper to me what you want to say." William still said nothing. Duane got up from where he was sitting and went over to stand with William on the stage, but still William said nothing.

After a while, a teacher in the audience said, "Maybe William just wants to say hello." We all burst into applause. Duane took William's hand, and they went back to where they had been sitting. The Earth Day assembly then proceeded, with the third-grade class deftly leading the class presentations.

In Chapter XXI of *The Little Prince*, when the fox is teaching the Little Prince how to tame him, author Antoine de Saint-Exupéry gives the fox what to me is one of the most important lines in literature: "Don't say anything. Words are the source of misunderstandings."[32]

> **"Words are the source of misunderstandings."**

The Earth Day assembly was wonderful. The third grade led it beautifully. They were a proud, disciplined group with a lot of important things to say. They let us know that bees have many uses in medicine; different bees have different responsibilities in a hive; honey tastes different depending on the environment of the hive; bees can get drunk from fermented nectar; the honeybee is the only insect that makes food for humans; and honeybees would rather not sting humans, because they are after something sweeter: the nectar. The other classes showed that they had been learning many important things, too. But what was truly remarkable about Earth Day was what didn't happen.

William didn't say anything. Christian didn't change the look on his face from loving confidence to worry. Duane did not speak for his buddy. None of the students started to squirm or titter or giggle. The teacher did not try to rescue William. Just think of all the things that didn't happen.

Mel Levine is the founder of All Kinds of Minds, a nonprofit education institute, and the author of many books about learning differences and what should go on in schools. He says, "All children in school are trying to maximize one thing above all others—and it is the same for all children. They are trying to avoid embarrassment."[33]

One of the most vivid memories I have from first grade is a particular show-and-tell. I remember even today how I felt as if I had actually been struck physically by embarrassment. The teacher had asked us to share jokes. I immediately put my hand up.

"Yes, Ricky. What is your joke?"

Instantly, I felt a little concerned. The joke I had thought of was a very common one. I was sure many people had heard it before. Nonetheless, I wanted to participate, even if my joke wasn't going to be a big hit. I didn't need to be a star; I just wanted to have something to say and join in. "Okay," I said. "Now, if any of you have heard this joke before, don't give the answer." Nods all around the circle. "Why did the chicken cross the road?"

Instantly, and without raising their hands, half of my colleagues jumped in loudly with, "To get to the other side," and everyone laughed.

I cried out, shouting over the hubbub, "I told you not to say it if you've heard it before," and then hunkered down into my shame and embarrassment.

For as long as I can remember, I have had the sense that I am not much of a joke teller. Others say that I have a good sense of humor and am always making people laugh, but fifty-seven years after this event, telling jokes remains firmly seated in my brain as "not me." My self-image does not include it. It is so easy for us to create labels, stories, attributions, and other generalizations about ourselves. Those responsible for our education need to keep undermining and transcending them.

Speaking up in front of others is one of the most important

things that your child does in school—not because every child needs to learn how to be a public speaker, but because speaking up and having his or her words (or wordlessness) accepted are critical to a person's sense of worth in the world. The ability to speak in front of others without embarrassment or shame is one of the prime predictors of success, right up there with delayed gratification. It is a fundamental skill, and yet the "back to basics" people never put it on the list of basic skills that schools should teach.

Speaking up matters, because your child needs to feel he or she has a voice. But paradoxically, creating an environment where students are encouraged to speak up requires having it be okay to say nothing.

# 28.

# Anatomy of a Miracle

∽

A person's behavior is more a function of the environment we create than of anything else. Lee Ross, a professor of psychology at Stanford University and co-author of *The Person and the Situation: Perspectives of Social Psychology,* points out that context is a better predictor of people's behavior than their moral compass. Whether someone lies or cheats or resolves conflicts with his or her fists is more a result of the situation he or she is in than whether or not he or she "knows better."[34]

Context is, of course, the result of many factors, like the culture of family, our community, our ethnicity, our nation, or the zeitgeist in which we live. Often overlooked is the context that each of us creates in our relationships. My child's behavior may very well be the direct or indirect result of my behavior, or the atmosphere I create, or even my own fears that I believe only I am aware of.

I call this the "Ackerly uncertainty principle," because it reminds me of Heisenberg's uncertainty principle, which (very loosely defined) shows that a human attempt to define an elementary particle—say, a photon—is dependent on how one approaches the particle. If we do an experiment to determine a photon's location (as if it were a particle), we cannot say anything about its momentum. If we do an experiment to measure the photon's momentum (as if it were a wave), we cannot know exactly where it is.*

I am aware that I would probably annoy Dr. Heisenberg if he knew how I apply his uncertainty principle to education, but I can't help it. The uncertainty principle always pops to mind whenever we talk about children as objective phenomena. The Ackerly uncertainty principle (critical for understanding human behavior) holds that a phenomenon cannot be understood apart from the method used for understanding it. In other words, we adults have a powerful effect on how our children seem to be.

Just as elementary particles like atoms are better understood as "quanta" than as discrete definable particles or waves, so children are better understood as bundles of energy that are impossible to fully understand than as definable beings. Children are not discrete, definable entities whose behavior is objectively predictable over time. Tests tell us mostly about the child in that testing situation. Neither are the diagnoses we give them particularly useful; they are often counterproductive.

We can, however, begin to predict our children's behavior when we engage in a scientific (or quasi-scientific) process of noticing how we cause it. I can notice that every time I say, "Time to put the ball away and line up," the child kicks the ball in the other direction. You can notice that every time you say, "Time to clean up your room," the child takes another toy off the shelf. If

---

*Physically, the uncertainty principle requires that when the position of an atom is measured with a photon, the reflected photon will change the momentum of the atom by an uncertain amount inversely proportional to the accuracy of the position measurement. The amount of uncertainty can never be reduced below the limit set by the principle, regardless of the experimental setup.

we can notice these things, we can begin to do experiments that produce the results we want, as in the example mentioned above of the sixth-grade teacher who renamed the dictionary "Huey."

Partway into my first year as principal, I found myself sitting across the table from a clean-cut, successful looking lawyer parent who two months before had put his beautiful blond daughter into the first grade of my school. We were at his downtown Kansas City club, the workday home of the social elite and apparently successful men. As soon as we had returned from the buffet, with plates full of samplings from the cornucopia of the affluent, he got right to the point. This was the gist:

"There is a boy in my daughter's class who is using bad language, who is bullying other children, and yesterday he destroyed her art project," he said. "Delia says his name is Richard. I don't know who he is, and I am sure you have to look after all of the students, and I am sure he has his own educational needs that you have to take care of, but I want you to know that I didn't move my daughter from the public schools to have her harassed by another student, and if you don't have this problem solved by Christmas, I will pull her out of your school."

This was no small threat. My mandate from the board of trustees was to keep this school from closing by providing the kind of education people like this would want to buy. The school was in a neighborhood that a real-estate agent had labeled with true Kansas City charm: "A little salt-and-pepper." It was 1974. Busing for racial balance had been imposed, and the whites were fleeing the public schools, against their core belief in the American way. I needed this man and his daughter to stay in the school, which was itself "a little salt and pepper" (38 percent students of color). I needed all the parents to know that their children were not only safe but also getting a good education.

My response to Delia's father was not very lengthy. I was completely new to the role of school principal. I simply said, "I will take care of it," without having much of an idea as to how, and with no conviction that I could be successful.

Of course, I didn't actually need a fire to be lit under me. It was quite unacceptable to me that Richard was behaving so badly in class. Everything that Delia's dad was reporting was exactly what the teacher had been reporting for a month. She and I had tried various interventions and punishments, and there had already been several conversations with his parents and notes back and forth from home, but nothing was working.

One Tuesday afternoon at 4 PM, mother, father, teacher, and I sat in my office to come up with a plan that would turn Richard's behavior around. However, at the end of an hour, we had still come up with very little. Then Joan, the teacher, thought to mention the fact that Richard was not in academic difficulty—in fact, he was very smart and a good learner. All of his academic skills were strong, and he was making good progress. Both parents smiled. The father visibly relaxed and began talking about his experience in school. In the course of this talk, he confessed that he had flunked out of second grade. "So this is great news," he said. "I have been so afraid that Richard would get kicked out of school, just as I was."

We talked for another hour, continuing to try to design a plan that would change Richard's behavior. At the end of two hours of talking, neither teacher nor parents nor I felt we had had any brilliant insights or had solved any problems. Nonetheless, we came up with a simple plan of consequences and agreed to be in communication with one another.

We never implemented the plan. We never had to. The next day there were no incidents. None the next, or the next, and the week ended with no more trips to the principal's office. In fact, there was no more bad behavior for the rest of the year, and the boy graduated seven years later in good standing. The disciplinary plan we established was never employed. Why?

The parents and teachers just became more disciplined about how they talked to each other. Richard's parents left our meeting with their fears markedly reduced. We felt like a team. The parents were convinced that neither teacher nor principal had it in for their child, and in fact wanted the best for him, and in fact were *not* considering kicking him out. Most important, the father was able to let go of his fears, which turned out to be the root cause (or among the root causes) of the undesirable behavior.

We didn't test the child for hyperactivity, attention deficits, "impulse control," or learning disabilities. We didn't threaten the child with expulsion or even suggest it to the parents. There was never any diagnosis, but I do have a sense of what we did right. With Richard it was:

1. We each came to believe that we all had one uncomplicated purpose: to help Richard. We each learned that this was true for all of us.
2. We saw ourselves as a team. We understood that Richard existed in a social system, and that each of us was a key determinant of the quality of that system. As a member of that team, each of us would play our position and trust that the others would play their position. We didn't even have our signals straight, and it worked.
3. Each of us had some power to make a difference, and yet none of us had the power to "fix" the "problem."
4. We shared information openly and honestly, especially information about ourselves.

5. We talked in specific terms about what we knew and didn't deal in labels, prescriptions, or generalizations, nor did we tell each other what to do.

6. By the end of the meeting, without knowing fully what each of us would do, we each believed that we all would be making our decisions in concert with one another.

7. We understood the fact that success was really out of our hands, and in the hands of Richard, and that we would have to count on him even though there was no evidence that we should.

Problems with kids aren't usually as easy to fix as they were with Richard, but often they are just that simple. Making a change in a kid is often a matter of reorganizing the village that is raising the child. That can sometimes be easy, and sometimes it is hard. What makes it easy is when the adults can work together to change themselves. What makes it hard is when one or more adults find it hard to change.

This incident taught me another principle. If you hear a statement that starts with the words "I'm afraid that . . .," you should take the fear seriously. Hundreds of incidents, piled on top of this one over the years, have borne this out. If

**If a parent is afraid, the child will pick it up.**

a parent is afraid of something about a child, the child will pick it up, even if there is a conscious attempt not to communicate it. The fear will find a manifestation in the child. This is how "the sins of the fathers" get "visited upon the sons."

We don't have to understand the situation. In the context of uncertainty, we have to start noticing the dynamic of which we are a part. Then we have to make ourselves free enough to stop doing what we usually do and start doing a little action-research on the problem with new behaviors. Then, usually in partnership with others, we will begin to create the conditions in which we increase the possibility that the behavior that needs to change will change. All such action-research starts with the assumption "I am causing it or allowing it to happen."

# VI: Staying Out of Trouble

# 29.
# Don't Throw Me in That Briar Patch

Jody told me about a conversation she had had with Michael, her five-year-old son. She opened it by saying that Michael is afraid he is mean.

> Michael: "Why am I so mean?"
> Jody: "Why do you say that?"
> Michael: "Because sometimes I do bad things."
> Jody: "You do bad things? Well, have you been sent to Mr. Rick yet?"
> Michael: "Oh, no. I am not that bad!"

Unfortunately, the "bad boy" concept is very well entrenched, about as entrenched as the concept of the headmaster as the terror that awaits all bad boys if they persist in their badness. I am sure that fear of the man behind the door will never disappear. (How many books or movies do you know in which the principal or headmaster is a good guy?)

A school principal is not a cop, or a judge and jury; he is an educator. Educators want education to take place. Trouble, or getting people out of it, may be the province of lawyers, but not of educators. Trouble is only what *character* has to go through to get somewhere. Avoidance of trouble pre-emptively or retro-spectively is bad for *character*. *Character* needs, values, and respects all aspects of reality, including boundaries and setbacks. So mistakes are to be valued as learning opportunities—and nothing else.

A principal's job is not so much to be *the* authority in the school, but to increase the authority of everybody else in the school and to make sure that overlapping authorities overlap harmoniously. Most of the time, my role is more one of coach than of cop. When it comes to students in my office, my questions are often these:

"What are you trying to do?"
"Did you make a mistake?"
"Why was it a mistake?"
"What will you do to fix it?"
"What will you do differently?"

That's about it. I do not want to hear a story; I do not want to hear about what someone else did. I do not want to hear about fairness, and I do not want an explanation of behavior. I do not ask why children did what they did, because I do not want an excuse or to invite them to say how someone else caused their behavior. I am looking for a simple sentence that begins with "I" followed by an action verb. This is because at the core of building character is taking responsibility.

**At the core of building character is taking responsibility.**

If a teacher wants me to talk to one of her students, it is because a student is unclear about one or more of these concepts and needs my help to clarify things. (Sometimes he or she just needs to know we mean business.) I am not being euphemistic.

To get the best results with kids, we need to change the paradigm in their minds about good and bad. For instance, I almost never ask the "normal" question: "Why did you do it?" They are expecting that one, and it only produces an excuse—and an excuse, if accepted, absolves the child of responsibility.

Owen was a boy who viewed the principal's office door as revolving. By the time I met him in the first grade, he had the game down:

**Phase 1:** See how close to the boundary you can skate without getting in trouble.

**Phase 2:** See how many reprimands you can get before the adult loses patience and the warnings turn into a punishment.

**Phase 3:** See how many punishments you can get before you get the ultimate: SENT TO THE PRINCIPAL'S OFFICE!

**Phase 4:** See how many different ways you can minimize the principal's punishment.

**Phase 5:** Take your punishment.

**Phase 6:** Go back to class and start over.

I hate for my door to revolve. I hate going round and round, getting nowhere. So as a principal who was new to the school but knew Owen's game, I had a conversation with Owen's mother about what I was seeing so far. She got mad and said, "He is not a troublemaker!!!"

"I know," I said. "I never said, 'troublemaker.' Do you think he is trying to stay out of trouble?"

"Of course!!!" she said, and kept talking.

I interrupted. "That's the problem."

"What do you mean, that's the problem?"

"I mean, if he is trying to stay out of trouble, he is not doing his job. You are not sending him here to stay out of trouble. You are sending him here to learn."

"Of course, but he also has to stay out of trouble."

"Yes, but he can't do both at once. If he is trying to stay out of trouble, he is not trying to learn, so his whole life will be about trouble or not. If we can get him to focus on trying to learn, he won't get into trouble—not in any big way. He will just make mistakes and fix them and move on like most people."

"That is what I am trying to do."

"I know, but it is not working. Let me tell you a story. It's about the 'acting as if' principle. It's about treating your child the way you would most hope he is, rather than the way you're afraid he is."

I went on. "When I was fifty, my daughter Katie taught me how to snowboard. At first I was fairly proud of how well I was able to manage, but halfway through the morning I started to get very frustrated. I could stand up, but I couldn't get the board to go where I wanted it to go. The harder I tried, the more frustrated I got. When I told her my problem, she said, 'Dad, it's easy. Look where you want to go and the board will follow.'

"Instant reward. I looked across the hill to where I wanted to go, and zip, off it went as if it had read my mind. One does not truly have to have faith. Often one simply has to act as if the myth is true, and sure enough it will happen.

"Owen is not a troublemaker. Owen does not have 'impulse control.' The myth we will believe is that Owen is a fine young man who is not yet the master of all his urges, ideas, and notions and that he has the capacity to learn from the right kind of negative feedback. Do not try to assess the accuracy of this statement. Do not start reviewing strengths, weaknesses, and imperfections. Do not get him tested. If we want to release Owen's full power constructively into the world, the starting point is to believe the myth. Then we do our part, which is to make it not in his self-interest to test the boundaries anymore.

"Owen has a lot of energy. He has been getting mixed messages, but if we persist and persist in concert with one another, Owen will show us that our prediction about him is correct. He's a great guy with a lot of imagination, energy, and drive who is just trying to make his way constructively in the world."

"But what if he does something bad?" Owen's mother asked.

"We will simply have a nice sharp consequence that you, your husband, and I have complete confidence in—something about which we are not ambivalent. It is best if it is a natural consequence rather than one he could talk us out of. We deliver it; then we get right back to business."

"This is going to be hard," she said.

"Yes, when they are younger it is easier. When they are older, sometimes they have experienced so much variety in boundaries that it takes a lot more work to place the fence where it needs to be and to electrify it. But he needs this."

Owen graduated two years ago. The headmaster of his high school told me the other day how happy they were that he is in their school.

But back to Jody and Michael. In playing the position of parent, Jody missed an opportunity when Michael said he was afraid he was mean. It would have been a good time to ask, "Why do you say that?" By asking this question, Jody could have taken the opportunity to find out what was really going on in Michael's heart as well as his mind—if Michael's saying that he was afraid he was mean was important information that needed parental exploration. What she said indicated that the important question for her was "Is he or is he not mean?"

Yes, some behavior is just plain wrong, and adults need to react to it simply and decisively—not much conversation about it, just consequences. And we should also keep trying to help kids make good decisions. To be effective in the world, children will get better results if they are kind, charitable, and collaborative. We want them to demonstrate these virtues, not only because it makes the world a better place but also because they will be happier this way.

But trying not to be mean will often perpetuate meanness. A kid won't stay out of trouble trying to stay out of trouble. Trying not to get caught being mean, for fear of being sent to the principal, will cause the principal's door to revolve. Since none of us with the responsibility of raising children want to play that game, we have to redefine the game and do things differently.

It is natural for a child of any age to break rules and do bad things. It is natural and a requirement that adults make sure they get their comeuppance. There is a part of them that wants to get caught. If they say "Don't throw me in that briar patch," throw them.

# 30.

# Getting Your Comeuppance

Usually, of course, bad behavior isn't motivated by evil. Children are more often than not truly innocent and naive. It is their natural tendency to try out all kinds of different behaviors. It is the natural consequence of having a good imagination—and a good imagination has important survival value whether you grow up to be a poet, or a scientist, or even a school principal. So children's propensity to try out new behaviors requires that schools and families be on their toes, ready to deliver a comeuppance so that a teachable moment will be educational.

Once there were three little girls, Kathy, Lilly, and Susan. When they arrived at my school, they were all seventh-graders from different schools. But in eighth grade, they turned themselves into a gang that was mean to other kids with increasing frequency and ferocity. Teachers knew it was happening but couldn't seem to catch the girls in a teachable moment or a punishable act. They were clever and slippery. The most we could do was talk to them. As you can imagine, that didn't change anything.

One afternoon, however, at the bus stop across the street from school, they approached Johnny, a sixth-grader with weak social skills. He walked with his head down, looking at his feet, his shoulders pulled over him like a turtle shell. By all accounts, including that of a teacher who watched the episode from a distance, the girls told Johnny to get up because they wanted to sit on the bench. He did. They mocked him for a while and then, as the humiliations built to a crescendo, one of the girls threw her half-finished Slurpee. It hit him in the chest and spilled banana-strawberry slush all down his front.

The witnessing teacher reached the scene just as the bus arrived, so she was not able to say much. But she reported the incident to me the next morning before the students arrived, so I was able to talk to the girls' homeroom teacher and have them come to my office as soon as they came to school.

I met with each girl, one at a time, in my office. Even though each had her own version of the incident, minimizing her own role in the affair, I sent them to class one after the other, telling them that their offense was serious and that I still had to consider what I would do about it. I also talked with Johnny, whose story corroborated the witnessing teacher's report.

I called Johnny's home and got his mother on the phone. "I am glad you called," she said. "Johnny told me all about it. The stuff was all over him. I was going to call you." I told her that I would check in with him and make sure he knew that I would keep him safe.

I called each of the girls' parents to tell them that I was going to suspend their daughters. (This meant that a parent needed to come to school and pick up his or her child as soon as possible.) In each case, I spoke with a mother. I got Kathy's first and said, "I will want Kathy to return to school as soon as I know that things are going to be different. When you think they are, call me, set up an appointment, come in with Kathy, and let Kathy convince me. If I am convinced, she can come back."

Kathy's mom was horrified, and after asking a few questions to get the facts straight she said, "Thank you. I'll talk with her and call you. Can I come now?"

"Yes," I said. "Give me half an hour to talk with her."

I said the same thing to the other two mothers. Lilly's mother, Loretta, was at work and asked if she could pick her daughter up at the end of the day. I said that was fine, and that Lilly would wait in my office until she arrived. Loretta was angry, but I couldn't tell if it was with me or with her daughter.

Susan's mother, on the other hand, came to her daughter's defense, asking if I was sure it had been Susan who had thrown the Slurpee. She wanted to know what the boy had done to provoke it, how I was disciplining the other girls, and what was being done about the boy. She concluded that I was overreacting, that this was way too small an offense to merit suspension.

Now, when I had told the girls they would be suspended, they hadn't said much. Not one tried to defend herself. The only way their behavior differed was the looks on their faces. Kathy's turned pale. Lilly looked afraid.

But Susan had a bit of a smile, radiant with arrogance.

True to her word, Kathy's mother was there by nine o'clock that morning. Susan sat outside my office until her mother came at eleven. Lilly waited in my office until five that afternoon. At 5:15, I got a call from Kathy's father, who asked if they could have an appointment first thing the next morning. "7:30?" I asked.

"Thank you," he said.

## Kathy

Kathy and her parents were at the door of my office at 7:30. Kathy sat directly across the table from me, with her parents in chairs to her right. She spoke first. Looking me straight in the eye, she said, "Mr. Ackerly, I know what I did was wrong. Even though I didn't throw the Slurpee myself, I was there and I didn't say anything. I laughed at what was happening, and I know we made Johnny feel bad. I know I was part of what made him feel bad. I feel bad about it, and I want to come back."

"Do you think that what you did was harassment?"

Pause. "Well, yes, sort of. I participated in harassment."

"Yes, you did. Can you think of anything you can do to fix it?"

With a thoughtful look on her face, she said, "I can't really fix it. But I can talk to Johnny."

"What would you say?"

"I don't know. I would say I'm sorry, but I know that wouldn't fix it, and I don't know what else I could do."

"But you would talk to him?"

"Yes."

"Is there anything else you can do?"

Long pause. "I can tell you that I will not harass anyone again."

"Can you guarantee that to me?"

"Yes." She looked down at the tabletop, and then back up into my eyes.

"Kathy, good job. I believe you. I want you to come back." Then I said to her parents, "Kathy can come to school today. You have a wonderful daughter here. You should be proud of her."

"We are," they said. It was five minutes past eight.


### Susan

Susan's mom called me mid-morning to tell me how inappropriate my handling of the situation was. She tried to clarify Susan's actions and asked a string of technical questions: "What does suspension mean? The handbook doesn't mention anything about calling kids names. She only threw a half-filled paper cup. She didn't hurt anyone. You say she can come back when you know that things are going to be different? What does that mean? How will you know? What are the criteria? What do you want her to say? What is she supposed to do to prove to you that things are going to be 'different'?"

The next day began with a call from Susan's mother: "Can we have an appointment?"

"Yes. When would you like to come in?"

"As soon as possible. My daughter needs to be in school. Don't you know that my daughter needs to be in school?"

"I can see you at nine o'clock."

At 9:15, Susan and both of her parents arrived in my office. Her mother sat directly across from me, her father to the right of her mother, and Susan off to the left, at the head of the table but a bit back from it, slouching in her chair. Her mom spoke first: "Susan wants to come back."

I turned to Susan and asked, "Do you want to come back?"

"Yes."

"Good. Talk to me."

"What? What do you want me to say? I want to come back."

"I don't want you to say anything in particular. I need to know that things are going to be different."

Susan's mom broke in: "Look, we talked to her. She doesn't think she did anything really wrong, but she admits that she threw the Slurpee and that it hit Johnny, even though she was just trying to throw it out and missed. But she says she knows it messed up Johnny's clothes and she is sorry. She assures us that she will be good. What more do you want?"

"Mrs. Pierce, this is not a court of law. I am not a judge. I am an educator. This is a school, and my responsibility is your daughter's education." Turning to Susan, I said, "I need you to take responsibility for what you did. I need to know that you are not going to harass other people. Susan, do you know that you have been mean to other kids?"

"Sometimes, but not more than anyone else. And sometimes people are mean to me."

"Can you tell me that things are going to be different?"

"I don't know what you mean."

Looking at both parents, I said, "Susan is not ready to come back. She cannot come to school today. Call me when she is ready."

"Look," said Susan's mother. "I am an adolescent psychologist. You are supposed to be an educator. Don't you realize it is normal for children to try out bad behaviors?"

"Yes, Mrs. Pierce, this sort of thing can happen. It is not abnormal for kids to be mean to each other. It is also normal for the adults to say no to it."

"Then you will not let her back?"

"Not until I know that things are going to be different."

The conversation was much longer than this, but there was nothing of substance said beyond what I have written here. Both parents stared at me in a rage, then popped out of their chairs like jack-in-the-boxes. By the time they gestured to Susan to leave, it was well past noon.

Susan and her family were back in my office the next afternoon after school—same seating arrangement. This time Susan spoke first. Still slouching in her chair some distance from the table, she said, "Mr. Ackerly, I know that what I did was wrong. I hit Johnny with the Slurpee. Please let me back in the school." The look on her face and tone in her voice said, "I know that this is what you want me to say, so I will say it."

"Did you do anything else wrong?"

"I called him names?"

"Will you assure me that you will obey the school rules and, in particular, that you will not be mean to anyone anymore?"

"Yes," she said, with that little smile on her face.

In my heart, I knew that nothing had changed inside her, but she had minimally done what she needed to do, and said what she needed to say. "All right," I said. "You can come back. But Susan, if you break any more rules, you will leave the school for good. I can't have anyone here who harasses people."

Neither Susan nor her parents said anything. Susan still had that confident little smile on her face as she returned to class.

In retrospect, I realize that I missed a trick. I should have asked Susan to make it up to Johnny and make sure that he felt she had made appropriate apologies and restitution. I doubt that it would have helped, though. It was obvious that the parents needed to change if Susan were to change. They and I would have had to form a tight partnership, to have come up with a strategy in which the three of us and the teachers each played carefully specified roles. We would all have had to commit to using new behaviors that we could all agree would help change Susan's. Each of us would have needed to know our lines, and we would have had to apply them consistently.

We needed to reorganize the little village that was raising the child. Could I have changed Mrs. Pierce in any way? Could I have worked with Mr. Pierce to make the change necessary? To all these questions I have to answer, "Perhaps." But honesty requires me to admit that I didn't like the way Mrs. Pierce spoke to me, and that I had no desire to help this child if her mother was going to be arrogant. Actually, I did want to help Susan, but I don't like wasting my time, and she didn't seem to want my help. Her mother only wanted me to let her be at the school; she didn't want Susan to get an education.

I had known things weren't going to be different, and they weren't. Susan's homeroom teacher, Karen, who also had her all morning for science and algebra and recess, saw me in the lounge after recess to say that Susan had been perfect all morning long. We began to congratulate ourselves. That was at 10:30. At 12:30, Karen and her partner teacher, Edie, stopped me at lunch to say that Susan had broken six school rules in the last two hours, that she had been completely contemptuous, and that she had topped it all off by spitting in the face of one of her classmates at lunch. She was sitting in my office.

I expelled Susan.

## Lilly

The day after I had suspended the three girls, Lilly's mother, Loretta, called to say, with exasperation and dismay, "Lilly is not ready to come back yet." (I knew Loretta, a single working mother, had probably had to stay home from work.) Then, after my first exasperating meeting with the Pierces, I listened to my messages as a way of depressurizing and heard Lilly's mother say, in a patient, resigned voice, "Lilly is still not ready to come back."

Lilly was out of school for that whole week and part of the next. On Wednesday I met with her and her mother in my office at 7:30. Lilly was appropriately contrite, made appropriate apologies to Johnny in my office, and said she would never be mean again. She said that she could not, however, promise that she would break no rules; there was still a lot of school year left. Her honesty was a good sign, and so this was also a right answer. I welcomed her back.

A month later, Lilly was back in my office, this time for being disrespectful to teachers. Before I could open my mouth, she burst into tears.

Nonetheless, I used my usual opening line. "Why are you here?"

She couldn't even answer through her sobs.

I said, "Not to worry. Take your time. I'll get back to what I was doing. Let me know when you can talk about this. Take your time." And I gave her a box of tissues.

Within a minute, she had calmed down enough to say, "It's not fair. Ms. Quinby is never fair. She doesn't like me."

"If I were to ask Ms. Quinby why you are here, what would she say?"

"That I was being"—she inserted an eye roll—"disrespectful."

"What do you think was disrespectful?"

"Nothing. I wasn't being disrespectful."

"I believe you, that you weren't *feeling* disrespectful. But what did you do that made Ms. Quinby feel disrespected?"

"Well, maybe," she said with the eye roll, "because I was talking while she was talking?"

"Yes, it could be that, but I know Ms. Quinby. That would not have been enough for her to send you to my office."

Silence.

"Was that the first time she picked on you this morning?"

"No. She has been doing it all morning."

"How many times?"

"I don't know."

"About five?"

"About."

"Well, that's it, then," I said, trying to hide my triumphant feeling.

"What do you mean?"

"She didn't send you to my office for talking. She sent you to my office because she was getting tired of having to talk to you about talking."

"But I was only . . ."

"Stop," I said. I was getting a glimpse of why it had taken her mother so long to bring Lilly back to school. "Look, I'll make a deal with you. Spend the rest of the week not talking when she is talking, and see if she keeps picking on you. On Friday, come to my office and tell me how many times she picked on you."

That was Monday. I didn't see her the rest of the week. Friday came, the weekend came, and Lilly didn't stop by. But I knew the problem wasn't fixed, just given a Band-Aid.

The next Tuesday, Lilly was in my office again. This time she came from mathematics class.

"Why are you here?" I asked, beginning the same drill as before.

"I don't know." No sobbing this time.

"But you keep being sent out of class."

"I don't always get sent out of class."

"Well, it is too many times for me. Let's have a talk with your mother. Maybe she can help me understand."

"No. Don't talk to my mother," she said, and now she did start to cry. "I won't get sent out again, I promise."

"Well, you go back to class and show me, but that doesn't mean we are not going to talk to your mother. She would not be happy to discover that you keep showing up in my office."

"Are you going to talk to her?"

"I haven't decided."

"Please, please, please, don't talk to her," Lilly pleaded.

"We'll see. You go back to class, and see if you can stay there."

I called Loretta as soon as Lilly left, relating the conversation, including Lilly's "Don't tell my mother." We decided that we would have a meeting when she came to pick Lilly up from school that afternoon.

As the meeting started, Lilly slouched in her chair in a pout. Loretta immediately snapped at her to sit up straight, which Lilly, getting angrier, did. We discussed the problem, but we all soon felt that we were getting nowhere; Lilly and Loretta were both locked in an angry prison. Finally, I said, "Lilly, do you feel under pressure?'

"Yes. Everyone is always on my case, and I never do anything."

"Do you think you need to be perfect?"

"Yes."

I smiled a big smile, leaned back from the round table at which we were sitting, and said, "I understand. You are acting as if you are in a different school."

"What do you mean?"

"I mean, here you don't have to be perfect—we don't want you to be perfect. We don't even want you to try to stay out of trouble."

"What?" asked Lilly, as Loretta tried to look unsurprised.

"No. You are playing the wrong game. You are here to make mistakes. Your mother is sending you here to make mistakes and to learn from them. If you never make any mistakes, you will never learn."

The expression on Lilly's face changed from tense puzzlement to relaxed openness, and she said nothing.

"Look, you need to change your mind about something. Here we don't want you to be perfect; we want you to learn. When you make a mistake, the important thing is not how bad a mistake it was, whether it was your fault or not, or whether it was even a mistake or not. The important thing is to turn it into a learning experience. We expect you to make mistakes. For the next week, I will give you a nickel for every time a teacher criticizes you and you receive it. Criticism is not a punishment; it is a gift."

Loretta said nothing. Lilly just looked at me, almost—but not quite—smiling.

"So here is the drill," I said. "At the end of tomorrow, you come see me and tell me how many mistakes you made that you admitted, and I will give you a nickel for each one."

"Is that it?"

"Yes, that's it. You come see me at the end of the day tomorrow, and collect your nickels and we will see how much you can earn this week, okay?"

"Okay."

## Follow-up
### Kathy

Kathy came up at a faculty meeting a month before graduation, as we were talking about awards, as a candidate for the citizenship award. One teacher said that it would be wrong to give it to a student who had been suspended. Another said that Kathy deserved the award, that she had proven herself to be the best citizen in the class by far. She had not only kept out of trouble, but had made many positive contributions to the community of the school. A debate ensued. I was very pleased with the outcome. One teacher who had remained silent for most of the discussion said, "Kathy should definitely get the citizenship award, and the fact that she made a mistake and corrected it is the main reason. We are here to make a difference, and we did. She showed in her behavior that she knew exactly what we are about and wanted to prove it to us. She has to get the award."

The vote was unanimous, and Kathy received the award for citizenship at graduation.

## Lilly

The day after I had asked Lilly to see me about the nickels, she didn't come, but I kept an eye out for her at dismissal. When I saw her, I asked, "How much do I owe you?"

"I made three mistakes," she answered.

I reached into my pocket, pulled out a dime and a nickel, and gave them to her. "See you tomorrow," I said.

She didn't come to see me on the following Thursday, either. But when I saw her at the end of the day, she said, with a big smile on her face, "You owe me ten cents."

"What for?"

"I interrupted Ms. Quinby twice."

"Okay," I said. "Here you go." And I gave her a dime.

But that was the end of it. There were no problems for the rest of the year. It was the best use I ever made of twenty-five cents.

## Susan

When I ponder the Susan situation, I still wonder what we could have done to help her. But I have learned that I am not the teacher for every child. Some people will get their education from others, not me.

Yes, we shouldn't give up too early or too easily. I have to keep acting as if my only limits are the limits of my imagination. At the same time, I have to remind myself that so much is out of our control. Some people never get educated. Of course, that is not something I like to contemplate. I am left with having to live and work in the tension described in the serenity prayer: "Grant me the courage to change the things I can change, the grace to accept the things I can't change, and the wisdom to know the difference."

When we are doing the job right, all of us—teachers, parents, and professionals alike—are confronted regularly with our powerlessness. There are some things we can change and some things we cannot. The quality of our decisions hinge on an accurate assessment of which is which—the essence of the art of playing position.

# VII: Good, Bad, and Integrity

*(Make Friends with the Monster
Under the Bed)*

# 31.

# Safe to Be Bad

❦

I think what has chiefly struck me in human beings is their lack of consistency. I have never seen people all of a piece. It has amazed me that the most incongruous traits should exist in the same person and for all that yield a plausible harmony.... The censure that has from time to time been passed on me is due perhaps to the fact that I have not expressly condemned what is bad in the characters of my invention and praised what is good. It must be a fault in me that I am not gravely shocked at the sins of others unless they personally affect me, and even when they do I have learnt at last generally to excuse them. It is meet not to expect too much of others.

—Somerset Maugham, *The Summing Up*

Jane, the mother of a three-year-old, e-mailed me the following story:

*Freddy and I were cleaning up his toys that were strewn about the family room. Let's just say he was an unenthusiastic participant. Finally, I set a limit, saying we would not be able to go outside until we finished putting his toys away. Soon afterward, he threw a toy at me, and it hit my hand hard. It hurt. I lost my temper and grabbed his shoulders and said in an angry voice, "You hurt me."*

*He was visibly shaken. He soon apologized for having hurt me. After a moment he said, "Mommy, the next time I throw my toys can you not grab me?" I told him that I was sorry for grabbing him so hard but explained that I had lost my temper because it really hurt when his toy hit my hand. I also said that I would try really hard not to grab him the next time I lose my temper. He seemed satisfied with this. So was I.*

*Later, when Marvin came home from work, I started telling him what had happened. Freddy chimed in, repeating to his daddy that he had asked me not to grab him the next time he threw his toys. At this point Marvin asked, "Freddy, why did you throw your toy at Mommy?"*

*Freddy considered the question. He then looked at his daddy and said, "Sometimes I just like to be bad." He waited a few seconds more and then asked, "Do you ever do that?"*

*I was hoping that Marvin would answer truthfully; I was not disappointed. Marvin said, "Yeah. I do, Freddy."*

*Then Freddy asked me, "Do you ever do that?" I answered, "Yeah. I do."*

*I was very moved by Freddy's ability to share his inner workings with his mommy and daddy. I hope we always have such intimacy! Interestingly, we had a great evening after that with no time-outs. Freddy seemed happy. I know I was.*

*—Jane*

When I talked with Jane and Marvin about this event, they confided their moral dilemma of whether or not to confess to wanting to be bad sometimes. Though each had had different upbringings, both had learned to deny their badness and were afraid that talking about it openly and honestly with Freddy would give him permission to be bad. They were both happy to discover that they had transcended their upbringings and found a better way.

In and out of school, this is something we adults all struggle with, but Jane and Marvin acted on to a solid principle of both a happy school and a happy family: Don't deny badness. If our schools and our families are to be strong, they have to be safe places to learn. We have to value moments we would rather avoid, including moments of conflict and badness. Facing badness can bring on very important learning. Human reality is largely made up of good and bad in just about equal measure, and to function properly, the reality-testing mechanism needs to know it all.

**Facing badness can bring on very important learning.**

Growing up, children are looking for a powerful adult (hopefully a parent) who can contain their badness—accept it, make room for it, yet not be destroyed or overwhelmed by it—someone who will neither withdraw from it nor retaliate. Children need adults who can accept badness as a fact of life and help them learn to work with it, to be creative with it, to play with it, and come to understand it.

I told Jane that it was good that she had apologized, in order to model good standards of behavior for Freddy; it is true that parents provide children with emotional security by being even-tempered in the face of upset. But I also told her not to feel too much guilt about having lost her temper. By doing so, even though she hated doing it, she had done something many adults have a hard time with: confronting a kid with the real consequence of his action.

This is a very un-1950s way of looking at society, but if people can accept badness as part of their realities, there will be less moralizing and more actual morality.

# 32.

# Violence and Evil

After reading my writing about Freddy on the DivineCaroline website, another mother e-mailed me her concern about violence in children:

> *My son's best friend told him yesterday that his dad was a boy soldier and fired machine guns when he was thirteen (could be true, as his dad is Cambodian). Now my son is fascinated by it all and thinks it's cool and wants to know if he'll get to fire one. I don't know how to react. So far, I'm downplaying it all and have only responded to his statement that Ben's dad was a boy soldier with "Isn't that sad." And to his, "Will I get to fire a machine gun?" I say "No, children aren't meant to be in armies; I'm sad Ben's father had to be in one." And then I changed the subject, and we started reading a bedtime story.*
>
> *I hope I'm handling this correctly. He's now making machine-gun sounds a lot when playing—and he's never seen or heard one, as we don't watch the news or any adult TV here—so that's come from his friend, too. Oy.*

My response:

*My short answer is: So far, so good. My longer answer is: It's important to neither over- nor underreact, and you didn't. That you are afraid puts you more at risk for overreacting, but what you said is perfect.*

*Your emotional tone is also important, and of course I can't tell that from your e-mail. Your focus should be calm, confident, sure of what would be dangerous and harmful, and sure of the reality of his situation. You can certainly tell him that real guns are not toys and way too dangerous in the same tone you would use to tell him not to eat something poisonous: "No. You don't want to do that. You could get killed." With most kids, all one has to do is point to a plant and say, "That's poison oak," and they won't go near it except by mistake, and then they will feel like idiots. If you overreact, they become intrigued. If a sign says WET PAINT, they have to test it.*

*At the same time, don't be afraid of boys making machine-gun sounds—or those of bombs or hand grenades, either. I don't know where we get it. It seems to be in the genes. I played soldier with toy guns from age five to age ten, and my favorite books and movies were about war. But playing war is a far cry from, and does not predispose or predict, a boy becoming a real warrior. In a "civilized" society, one of the challenges boys face is how to be their warrior selves constructively. So don't let your fear of war cause you to overreact and try to drum the warrior out of your son. That could have negative side effects.*

*Your best role is to be someone he can count on to tell him the truth about the world. Your best focus is to be sure of what you know and be ready to stand with confidence* when your knowledge and beliefs get tested. (It is the child's job to test them.) It sounds like you passed this test but are nervous about other tests to come.

**Be someone he can count on to tell him the truth about the world.**

For future tests, it's important to remember not to lecture. A smart parent waits for the right moment to drop one or two good lines (just as you did). Don't rant. Rants are bad because your child reads them as confusion rather than confidence. A voice in him says, "If Mom was sure of what she is saying, she would say it simply and calmly. She is clearly upset about something. I am not sure what, but she clearly has issues."

At this young age, there's no need for much detail. So if your child continues to pretend he has a machine gun, try saying, "I know too many tragedies that have come from guns, and there is no really good reason to have one, so in my house, guns are out." Some parents rule out toy guns, also. I don't think that is necessary, but if you can do it without sounding overreactive, go ahead.

Violence is one of those realities of life we have to be careful of—as with hurricanes and earthquakes, it's bad to go overboard trying to prevent it from ever happening. That kind of striving for the impossible can make things worse. We certainly need to continue to reduce violence in the world. We need to find better ways of resolving conflict. But your son will come to understand the horror of violence through natural processes. It doesn't all depend on you.

It is often a good idea to talk your positions over with a friend or your husband or the father of your kids. It is best if all the adults working with your child are on the same page, *but this is not always possible and is also not necessary. Children can adapt to a world that is not homogeneous and consistent. (They have to; it isn't.) The important thing is your confidence.*

*I hope this helps, Rick*

Violence and evil are in the world and in us as well. Each human being carries both around with them. Denial of evil and violence usually results in evil and violence. In fact, evil is not so bad; it's fear of evil that is. Most of the stories in this book are about how the exercise of certain disciplines has changed things for the better in the lives of certain children. But there are children I am still worried about, because changes that need to be made in their environment are not being made.

I worry about Clive, because his parents don't know how to—and/or are afraid to— require socially responsible behavior. One set of divorced parents continues to protest that their son, Demetri, is a good kid, and that I don't like him and have labeled him as a bad kid—pure projection, because I indeed like him very much and don't ever label kids "bad." Gregg, whose parents keep insisting that his antisocial behavior is the result of a learning disability and therefore must be tolerated, is still not learning what he needs to learn in order to harmonize his interests and needs with those of his classmates. Billy's parents heed his therapist, who claims that his problem is that his frontal lobes are dissociated from his limbic system, and say that therefore he cannot be held to the same standards as the other students. I could easily name half a dozen other children whose bad behavior was a direct result of the parents' attempt to eliminate evil or violence from their child.

Fairy tales often have a lot of evil and violence in them. Because of this, some adults would rather not read them to children, but this is misguided. Most fairy tales are stories about how our hero (or heroine) in*geniu*sly (note the spelling) integrates evil into his or her journey toward wholeness. Fairy tales are age-old, time-tested methods for educating the soul. A good fairy tale helps us metabolize our evil.

Parents can make mistakes on both sides of evil. We need neither to deny it nor to fear it. The disciplines most likely to help our children to deal with evil effectively are those that help us with our own growth. Naive innocence: believing or pretending that evil does not exist creates a space for evil to enter the world. On the other hand, being afraid gives it too much power. Being afraid makes it harder for us to stand up to it, and to help our children to stand up to it. Talking with our kids about it is not as important as becoming aware of our own weaknesses with respect to evil, because our kids will likely just pick up on our true stance vis-à-vis evil no matter what we say.

Fear no evil.

# 33.

# The Discipline of Patience

Character development is not about becoming a good person, but about being one's unique self more effectively.

"Five minutes to dinner, darling. Get ready. Five-minute warning, okay?" Margaret did not holler this to her son, Jimmy, from the kitchen. She took the trouble to go into the living room, where he was playing on his Game Boy. She was careful to get a look-me-in-the-eyes acknowledgement.

So when, five minutes later, she said, "Okay, put your game away now. It is time for dinner," it was appropriate for her to expect a pretty quick reaction. She did not, however, get it. She got nothing. She decided to be patient; she likes being a patient person. Although she found herself moving from annoyed to peeved to angry, she restrained herself from saying anything.

I know so many patient parents like Margaret, and it is not a bad way to be, but this exercise of patience is not always that good for kids. For a child to ignore a mother who has been working hard in the kitchen to get dinner on the table is to do violence to her. This is a good battleground for standing up to violence. To treat this behavior with "patience" is to collude in tyranny. Anger is an appropriate response to being treated with contempt.

Peace of mind can come from how we exercise our patience and how we express our anger. Grace comes not so much from a commitment to being grace-ful as from the acquisition and practice of skills, careful use of language, and the exer-cise of spiritual disciplines.

**Anger is an appropriate response to being treated with contempt.**

What are our options under these circumstances? We could brainstorm a list. Here is a starter list of not-so-good options:

- Go into the living room, grab him by the ear, and pull him into the dining room.
- Threaten to throw his dinner on the floor.
- Go into the living room and take the Game Boy out of his hands.
- Yell, "Jimmy, I told you dinner is ready!"
- Go ahead and eat without him.
- Tell him if he doesn't come now, he won't get any dessert.
- Say, "I am going to count to five. If you are not in your seat on five, you will do the dishes alone; on six, you will do them for two nights; on seven, three ..."

Not so good. But at least we are thinking. We could also get what we want without getting mad—in fact, we could make everyone laugh and get what we want at the same time:

"Okay, we could go through the usual drill. I say, 'Time for dinner'; you ignore me; I raise my voice and say it a second, then a third time; you underreact with something like 'Uh huh.' Then, when nothing happens and you are still playing your game, I make a threat, and then you get mad at me for threatening, and then I get mad for you getting mad, when I gave you plenty of warning and the unpleasantness is your fault anyway. Then I yell at you one final time and say that you are going to bed early and get no TV tonight, and then you storm into the dining room and slam your body into the chair, and then we start eating, and nobody says anything for a while . . .

"*Or*, we could just save ourselves all this trouble, and you could just put the game down and come to dinner now. Under this scenario, you would enjoy the dessert I have planned, and we could have some fun together after dinner, and be happier all at the same time. What do you say?"

We are smart enough to know that there is going to be a game. If we don't want to play it, we can name it and suggest another game. In other words, maybe this is not a time for patience but cleverness. It does seem that some strange combination of political correctness, pop psychology, and affluenza has caused Americans to think that it is actually possible as well as desirable for our children to be happy all the time and for the adults to be constantly "nice." Several years ago, I was talking with the mother of two children whose father had just left them. In talking with me about her concerns for her ten-year-old son, she said, "I just want him to be happy."

"That is probably not a reasonable objective right now," I said. "His parents are getting divorced, for heaven's sake. They are fighting with each other. That same fight is going on inside him. Happy? Does that make sense?"

"No, I guess not."

"Trying to make him happy will only make things worse. You and he need to share your anger and your grief with each other. Could it make sense to your children for their mom to be happy right now? Should it? Maybe this is an opportunity for all three of you to practice dealing with negative feelings."

Children need to be able to express anger, disappointment, sadness, and grief in an emotionally safe environment. While it is true that parents provide children with emotional security by being even-tempered in the face of upset, still there are a number of things, such as acts of disrespect and contempt, that should make an adult angry. Seeing what makes their parents angry, happy, and sad is also an important component of the development of children's emotional intelligence.[35] And seeing a variety of constructive ways of expressing negative feelings can be very important in preparing children for life.

Just as it is better for a child to work at being true and loving instead of trying to be "good," so, too, it is better for adults to work at being true and loving, rather than trying to be "good parents." Watching children do things that are hurtful or annoying to themselves or others without any emotional reaction is not in the interests of the child or society.

Furthermore, it is not that constructive to see patience as a personality trait. I say, "Personality, smersonality." Sure, you have your personality—a flawed one; we all do, and we all have to challenge ourselves to learn the disciplines to mitigate the negative effects of whatever personality that is.

Patience is better understood as a discipline that a person can acquire for the sake of the children. All personality types— quiet and loud, even-tempered and volatile—can be both true to themselves and effective with their children by exercising disciplines like patience gracefully.

# VIII: Let Them Teach You

*(Be Open to Learning about Yourself
as You Teach Your Children)*

# 34.
# What Would Be the Smart Thing?

Many years ago, when I was getting ready to put six-year-old Peter to bed, I noticed that there was a two-hour TV show that I wanted to watch, which I would miss because of his bedtime. I irresponsibly said, "Peter, would you like to stay up late and watch TV with me? Or would you like me to read you a story and put you to bed?"

He said, "Dad, what would be the smart thing to do?" In the nicest way, he played Solomon to me. So you see, it's been like this ever since Brooke took her walk.

When I have told this story, as I have many times since, people find it unusual that a six-year-old would have this response to such a question, and they don't imagine that their child would react the same way. The point of the story, however, is not to recommend an approach to children, or to suggest that children can be counted on to act in certain ways. On the contrary, the point is that children can surprise us. If we are open to the surprise, we can let them educate us. Peter reminded me of one of the most important educational imperatives: Let the children lead us. Listen to them; look deeply into what they say and do; use them to help us help them.

THE GENIUS IN CHILDREN

We also must use children to help us look into ourselves. For it is in ourselves—selves willing to change—that we will find solutions to our persistent problems. After all, it was a child who said, "The emperor has no clothes."

There is a subtheme in my story about Peter and bedtime, and that is that there are appropriate roles for parents to play and appropriate roles for children to play, and that these roles are different. In fact, in the little "villages" that raise children, everyone has to play position. The domain of decision-making required by each of the players in a child's life is quite different. Leading the child's character out into the world so that it can function effectively and gracefully within it requires shared decision-making, and

**Pay attention to where one person's authority begins and another person's ends.**

effective shared decision-making requires that everyone has an idea of where one person's authority begins and another person's ends.

Often, each of us knows at some level when we are "out of position." Peter knew that I was asking him to make a decision that was really mine to make. I knew it too, but I was being lazy. Somewhere inside of most adults and children is a knowledge that informs us of when people are playing position and when they are not. We do not always give voice to it. Perhaps most children, when given the opportunity to stay up past bedtime to watch TV, would simply say yes to a question like the one I asked Peter. But the wisdom exists, regardless of age, and for best results with our children, we should listen to that wise inner voice, notice when our children are listening, and open ourselves to learning.

My four children, the sum of whose ages is now approaching 139, have been, and continue to be, instrumental in my learning. Knowing that this is one of their functions in the world has been most helpful. In the first place, it has made me a better father. Second, it has helped me properly process the pain they cause me as well as the pain that I cause them. Third, seeing the job of parenting as a learning experience has made me a better person not only in the moment, but also in the future, as the lessons I learn sink in, one event at a time. Finally, my children keep bringing me back to my own genius.

My father knew this. On May 15th, 1978, I received a thank-you note that my father wrote after he returned home from his first visit to see his second granddaughter, Lizzie, who was then three weeks old. It included the following sentence: "It was so nice to meet the person who will complete my son's education." Indeed!

# 35.

# Making Mistakes

When Brooke went on her by-now-famous walk, I was a young parent—all of twenty-two years. I am proud of how I handled that moment in the woods in the summer of 1967, but I could point to many moments I handled badly, out of either ignorance or stupidity or misguided practices inherited from my own parents. At first I thought that raising a child was like training a dog—the way my father trained dogs, that is: When they do something you like, you reward them; when they do something wrong, you spank them.

Brooke was three years old the last time I spanked her. I had picked her up at the day-care center after a day of teaching. I was as thrilled to see her as she was to see me. She ran at me, all eyes, teeth, arms, and legs, and leaped into my arms.

As we hugged and kissed, the teacher came up to me with panties in a baggy, saying, "Brooke made a little mistake." My heart sank, as I knew that I had to break up this love-fest with a spanking. She cried all the way to the car, into the car, and all the way home. My heart broke. It was so broken that by the time I got home, I had determined that I had to get advice. Luckily, our next-door neighbor was a school principal.

That evening I went over to his house and asked if we could talk. As we walked around the block in our small, leafy town of Orange, Virginia, he said, "Oh, Rick, you don't have to do that. Kids naturally train themselves. They want to grow up. They don't want to keep wetting their pants. They want to be big and control themselves. All you have to do is support it. You certainly don't have to spank them."

I was so relieved. I had thought I was doing what a parent was supposed to. I never spanked Brooke again. She toilet-trained herself and went on to become a professor of feminist political theory at Vanderbilt University. I had needed some advice, and I got it when the need was great enough. Brooke's agonized crying resonated in my heart; I had to make a change.

All sound advice to parents can be summed up in three imperatives:

1. Provide unconditional love.
2. Strengthen children as decision makers.
3. Define and enforce boundaries (. . . and find better ways than spanking to enforce boundaries).

There. Three principles, nicely and simply delivered. People are complicated, however, and following this excellent advice becomes trickier and trickier as we grow. Psychologists will tell you that the parent-child relationship alone carries the baggage of many generations—enough to throw us off track. We make mistakes because most of the time we are not acting according to principles like the ones stated above, but according to practice.

In the early days of my parenting, I acted more or less the way I had been acted upon. These patterns are often very resistant to change. Luckily for both me and Brooke, that was not true in this case; I was willing to learn and to make myself new.

# 36.

# Who's Going to First Grade?

One spring a mother was chatting with me in the courtyard beside the school. She told me that she was going to visit chapel on Friday so that she could help her son, Jacob, who would be entering first grade in the fall, "adjust to coming to St. Luke's."

She was, of course, welcome, and her request was all the more reasonable since she was Jewish. I did, however, have the presence of mind to say, "Does he know he is coming to St. Luke's?"

"Yes," she said.

"Then he is already adjusting on his own."

She said, "I know, but he is Jewish and has never been to church before. I imagine that much of it will be strange, and I would like to see for myself so that I can prepare him for what he will be experiencing."

She had more to say on the subject, and after listening carefully I said, "I understand your position. I know I am being presumptuous, but may I suggest to you that you ask yourself the question, 'Who is it that is going to first grade?'"

To her credit, she did not get defensive, but said, "I know what you are saying. It is something that I need to do. I have to let Jacob live his own life. But it is also very hard. I hope you will work with me on it."

"Of course," I said, and work on it we did in the course of the next eight years. The issue came up again and again in different forms:

"Whose homework is it?"
"Whose disability is it?"
"Who is having trouble adjusting socially?"
"Who is going to high school next year?"

Once I found myself asking, "Why do you say, 'We had trouble with our homework?' I mean, you keep saying, 'we.'"

Again, she correctly took it as a rhetorical question and responded with, "I know. You are right. I meant to say, 'He had trouble with his homework.'"

There were many such discussions, long and short, in the course of those eight years. Some of them were very challenging for both of us and for the teachers who worked with her son. Some were painful, but we remained friends through it all. Luckily, she and I both saw this as part of the process of education. I learned at least as much as she did in those eight years.

She was not a slow learner; she was very smart. She just had a high mountain to climb, and she knew it. Once, when Jacob was in eighth grade and I was driving him and three friends back from a museum, I overheard him say, "My mother is *totally* overprotective."

Eight years later, we were both congratulating her son on his success at getting into the most challenging independent school in the city. At graduation she said, "Again, Rick, you proved the Ackerly theory is correct."

Unaware that there was such a thing, I asked, "What is the Ackerly theory?"

"The child knows," she said, and Ackerly theory number 1 was born. It is, simply stated, that if we act as if the child knows,

207

as if children have wisdom within them that guides them inexo-

**The child knows.**

rably toward being the human beings they were meant to be, we will be doing the best we can in creating the conditions for our children's success.

In the subsequent twenty years of raising children and being the air-traffic controller for thousands of other people's children, the theory hasn't really changed much. What has changed is that I have seen this theory in action in so many different ways, and have found so many different words for and manifestations of the inner wisdom of the child: character, soul, teacher within, destiny, calling, and genius.

We all need to grow, if children are to grow. Acting as if we have our own teachers within can help us see clearly enough to see the genius of our own children.

# 37.

# Who's Saving Whom?

Watching our children with our hearts as well as our minds is necessary in order to find the balance we need as we surf the waves of teaching children. Children are showing us truths about themselves all the time. We would be well served to listen to them, and listening to them is an art, not a science.

Victoria was walking with her four-year-old daughter, Lizzie, down by San Francisco Bay after a storm. The wind had veered around to the northeast and made their jackets fly as they skipped along, dodging around and stepping into puddles. Pink clouds scudded across the twilit sky.

After one particular gust, Lizzie said, "Mom, if a big wind came along and blew me up to that cloud, what would you do?"

"Hmmmmm," said Victoria. "Well, I would look around for the biggest ladder in the whole world and climb up there and get you."

"No. That wouldn't work. The ladder might hit me in the head."

"Okay, then," said Victoria, "I would get a very long rope and make a lasso, and whirl it around and around and throw it up to the cloud and catch you with it and bring you back down to me."

"No, that wouldn't work. The rope might get me around the neck and choke me."

"All right, then. I would get in a rocket ship and launch it up to the cloud so that I could come fetch you safely back down to earth."

"But the rocket ship might punch a hole in the cloud and make it fall down, and I would die."

"All right, then," asked Victoria, "how *would* we get you back down?"

"That's easy," said Lizzie. "I would hop to the next cloud up, and then the next one, and then the next, and then the next all the way up to heaven. There I would borrow some wings and flutter all the way back do the earth."

In the stories she was telling, Victoria was trying very hard—and brilliantly, we might add—to save her daughter. In the end, Lizzie recognized that she had to save herself. Deep in any mother's psyche is the need to communicate her love for her child, a love intent on saving her life. Deep in any child's psyche is the knowledge that it is all up to her. In the eleven years that I have watched this relationship develop, this dynamism has been the engine for self-discovery for both Victoria and Lizzie. As their geniuses dance together, the experience is almost mystical.

Lizzie, now age fifteen, went off to camp last week. She sat on her mother's lap, making like she was four years old again. They talked, cooed, and chortled with each other for a good hour. However, when the doorbell rang and it was time for her to leave, Lizzie marched out the door with a wave and a smile that communicated how thrilled she was to be off on her own, kicked off by a fest of pure love. The purpose of the love-fest was to communicate this: "I know that you know that I love you, and you know that I know that you love me, and it is as perfect now as it always has been."

A child's inner wisdom that it is ultimately "up to her" has a deeper dimension, too. A child's natural inclination is different from that of the parents. The parent's priority is for the child to be safe; a child's focus is to be somebody. It is as if there is a voice inside her that says, "Sure, I could stay alive, but what would be the point? What am I staying alive for?" Kids act as if they are pursuing the purposes of their lives. They do not act as if they are simply trying to stay alive. It's as if they are ready to say at any turn, "Mom, what's the point? I have work to do. I have to be about this business. I can't tell you what it is, but I am determined to find out. Let me go."

One thing I have learned from being a teacher and a father is to feel and live in one of the great paradoxes of parenting: Although I am in charge, sometimes the best way to exercise that charge is to let the children show us. When one-year-old Brooke went on her little walk, I was educating her, even though all I did was watch carefully, make sure the environment was safe, and not interfere. Victoria was educating Lizzie, even though she was only creating the conditions in which Lizzie would come up with the solution. Even though I behaved badly during one of Peter's bedtimes, Peter got a bit of an education by asking me a question and being right.

It is most important to note, for Gail (the one who likes *The Nanny*) and all the Gails among us, that in all these cases, the adults didn't figure anything out in advance; they just did what seemed like a good idea at the time and then adjusted their behavior as the children gave the signals. The thinking follows the behavior more often than not.

First position in the dance of helping our children learn is to notice, to value, to delight in, and to wonder at these moments, and most of all to be on our toes. Keep a watch out, because the lessons often come when you least expect them.

# 38.

# Being True to Your Genius

Raising a child, of course, has no end. One of the special challenges of being a teacher is that you never know when to declare success. Very few of the lives whose stories informed this book are over. How then are we to measure success? If there is no way to do so, how do we know that one approach is better than another? Triumphs occur. Will this string of successes last, or is this a "one-hit wonder?" Should we take responsibility for the successes? Watch out. We might have to take responsibility for the failures . . . and of course we have almost no control over these feelings. Disasters occur. We will feel guilty. We will blame ourselves. If we are good parents, we are in the habit of taking responsibility, and that brings with it the feeling of fault even if there is no link—a complete accident of biology or physics.

So what we are left with is to ask ourselves if we played our position as well as we could. Much of this has already been covered, but here are few extras that you may already be expecting based on what you have just read.

**Begin a Sentence with "My Conscience Requires . . ."**
For myself, I have learned that to sleep at night, I have to feel that I did a good job today. How do I know? Part of the answer

is that I behaved with integrity. When I wake up at four in the morning, turn on my radar screen, and am full of doubts—which is almost every night—I often go over what happened and what I could do differently tomorrow. If I remember a moment about which I could say that at least I did the right thing, that is what success looks like. Perhaps I think of how I could say to someone—or even did say to someone—"Well, I know it hurt, I know you are having a hard time with my decision, but my integrity required it." Sometimes I can even say to myself, "I couldn't in good conscience do anything else." Perhaps I even had the presence of mind to begin a sentence with "My conscience requires . . . ." Sometimes that's the best we can do. Were we granted the courage to change the things we could change, and the grace to accept the things we couldn't change, and did we accurately assess the difference?

## Use Fear as a Warning Device

We need to find disciplines to help us deal with fear, because fear will almost always separate us from our genius and make us do ineffective or destructive things. Out of fear, we make desperate, shortsighted lunges toward the target rather than taking the long view and taking careful, wise aim. We forget what we know and act out of habit. In fear we are held hostage to our obsolete cultures—their habits, their rituals, their folk wisdom, their practices—and collude in perpetuating them. Fear keeps us frozen in the past, afraid that change will make things worse instead of better. Fear shortens our horizon, narrows our vision, and reduces our behavior to broadly popular, commonly acceptable practices, rather than letting us think and act creatively and flexibly in the moment.

In fear we lose patience with children and stop treating them as if they know what they are doing. We are afraid to confront them with the requirements of the environment and with our own requirements, because we are afraid that "no" will hurt their self-esteem. In fear children hunker down and try to stay out of trouble, instead of engaging with abandon in the pursuit of knowledge; they try to measure up instead of striving for greatness. Fear makes them try to be perfect instead of taking the risks necessary to be great. Fear can make kids doubt themselves.

Fear keeps us from opening up to the learning opportunities inherent in error, failure, disappointment, struggle, loss, and conflict. We protect our children and ourselves from these things. We are afraid of our weaknesses, of our "failings," of our "character flaws," and, most deeply, of being wrong, that our way of constructing the world is wrong—it is fundamentally a terrifying prospect. We are afraid of diversity for *all* of the above reasons. In fear our relationships become confrontational power struggles. In "real life," winning, or at least not losing, may be very important, even though we know that winning *over* the other person is usually shortsighted.

Therefore, we must use fear as a warning device—one warning us not of something "out there," but of something inside. We need to use fear to alert ourselves that we are about to do a stupid thing. Then we stop, notice, and think of the smart thing to do—the thing that will make the desired difference. But we should never act directly out of fear.

**Act as If . . .**
There is the "act as if" discipline, as in: Act as if your child wants to learn. Don't wonder if it's *true*. Act as if your partner is the way you would most fondly hope he or she would be (ignoring evidence to the contrary). Act as if you caused or allowed some-

thing to happen, even though, of course, you didn't. Act as if that other person is not out to get you, which is different from dropping your guard. Act as if you are the variable (and your child and everyone else are the constant). Act as if the child knows, even though it is obvious how little he knows. This is not the same as "Be optimistic," or even "Be positive." You can and should keep going on basing your decisions on facts—always be a realist. The "act as if" discipline is based on the fact that if you don't act as if things will go the way you want them, you can be pretty sure they won't.

Then, of course, there is the most important one: Act as if your child has a genius, even though there may be very little proof.

### Stop Every Fifty Minutes and Admire Your Work

Once when I spent a week building a cabin in the woods with my friend Mike, I learned one of the great secrets of life. As he worked, he channeled his father, who had also been a builder: As he did things, he would recite his father's slogans. For instance, as he was measuring a board in preparation for cutting it, he would say, "Measure twice, cut once." As he sawed his way through a board, he would say, "Get your body aligned and you won't have to work so hard." As he drove a nail home with his hammer, he would say, "It's all in the wrist," and so on.

I guess to be a disciplined builder one should remind oneself of the disciplines. I don't know if that is necessary for building, but I do know that it is necessary for education. So many of the disciplines required for education are not normal behaviors.

Of Mike's father's little sayings, my favorite was "Stop every fifty minutes and admire your work." This is definitely not something I would naturally do, and I found it was very helpful in a variety of ways. Resting, of course, is a good thing. It gives you a chance to take a drink of water and maybe a chocolate-chip cookie. Also, I discovered, as I took a few minutes to look at my work, that I looked at it from a new perspective, and from a new perspective I often discovered that had I continued as I was going, I would have messed up. More times than I ever would have thought, I found that I brought to my work a new idea of how to proceed that was always more efficient, or more elegant—or less klutzy than I would have pursued had I just gone on as I was intending before the break. Most important, though, I was giving myself a spiritual boost. My friend's father's saying was not "Take a break once in a while"; it was "Stop every fifty minutes and *admire* your work."

As I said, one of the challenges of raising and teaching children is that we so rarely see the results. We don't really know how we are doing for years or lifetimes later. Reminding yourself to admire your work every day can help with this. Since we can't evaluate the quality of our work now by some benchmark achieved in the future anyway, one thing we can do is evaluate it in the moment. Stopping every fifty minutes to admire our work gives us a chance to look at what really matters, and that is the quality of our relationship now.

We can take stock of the state of our genius, and "in the moment" is the best time to do this. If we simply stop and notice, we can see it every time. With perfect accuracy we can feel delight, enthusiasm, inspiration, greatness, integrity, compassion, authenticity, humor, grace, beauty, truth, justice, playfulness, and fun. These are all valid and accurate measures of the state of our soul, and our own inner clarity is the most direct route to doing or saying the right thing, which might often be nothing.

It is, therefore, often perfectly easy and perfectly accurate to assess the quality of our work with our children, if we just stop and admire our work.

# Epilogue:
# Mantras for Working with Children

Since any list of principles and disciplines of maximizing learning is fairly arbitrary, I am free to select five that you can take away with you as mantras . . . and you will a need a mantra or two. They will stand you in good stead if you can remember them, and so I have constructed a handy way for you to keep them always handy.

Clench your hand into a fist and recite the following five four-syllable sentences, extending one finger for each.

1. Let Them Struggle
2. Love, Don't Label
3. Fear No Evil
4. Let Them Teach You
5. Play Position

When you are done, you will find that your hand is open and ready to be extended to your child, ready to be of service if necessary.

## 1. Let Them Struggle

Struggle, failure, mistakes, disappointment, and loss are opportunities. Missteps, mishaps, and mistakes on this journey are vital to growing up strong. If a child's genius is engaged, the trouble can strengthen him or her, and the child will often persist through failure.

## 2. Love, Don't Label

Generalizing is a threat to education. Parents and teachers can get distracted as a child fails to measure up to the requirements of the environment. Beware of diagnosis. Labels, attributions, diagnoses, generalizations, and the whole idea of "normal" can be distractions and can be dangerous. "Normal" is the enemy of genius.

## 3. Fear No Evil

Make friends with the monster under the bed. Evil loves a vacuum. Your child needs to know that you are strong enough to say no without having to retaliate, annihilate, withdraw, or abandon. Bad behavior must be confronted, and damage must be prevented. At the same time, we must come to accept, forgive, and metabolize evil into ourselves rather than to attempt to exterminate it.

## 4. Let Them Teach You

Be open to learning about yourself as you teach your children. Children can actually save us from ourselves. If we decide that the business of education begins with our own education, we have a fighting chance of changing so that our fears don't come true.

## 5. Play Position

It's the first and last set of disciplines. You can't solve all the problems or be everywhere at once. Other people are going to have to take responsibility in their appropriate sphere.

# Appendix

A sampling of disciplines that might be found in this book.

**A.** Do the present right. (The future will take care of itself. Let go of the outcome.)

**B.** Expose the gap. (Don't pretend that our behavior measures up to our principles.)

**C.** Treat them as if they know what they are doing.

**D.** Say: "Show me that you are ready." (We don't actually know if they are ready to take responsibility. Don't assume; make them commit.)

**E.** Take responsibility. Always notice how we cause the thing we hate or allow it to happen, even if it seems that we didn't.

**F.** If we care more about something (say, homework) than the child does, we absolve the child of responsibility.

**G.** Say no. ("No" does not hurt your child; the absence of boundaries does.)

**H.** Keep your eye on the long haul and the whole child. (Don't get obsessed by short-term shortcomings.)

**I.** Work on telling the truth gracefully. (Not: "Be positive and avoid the negative.")

**J.** Instill the habit of open self-evaluation. (Not: "Nothing succeeds like success." Don't hide your gap from others.)

K. Support them in learning through struggle, disappointment, loss, failure, conflict, strangeness, and change. (Do not avoid these.)

L. Remember: Engaging with reality is what builds a child's self-confidence—not praise.

M. Act as if you are the variable (and your child and everyone else is the constant).

N. Be present and empathetic (but don't interfere with natural consequences).

O. Deal in accurate anecdotes, details, and other directly observable data. (Avoid diagnoses, labels, and generalizations of all sorts. Don't ask, "Why?" so much.)

P. Look for uniqueness and value difference. (Stay away from "normal.")

Q. Strive for greatness (not excellence, not standards). Never compare.

R. Stand up to evil and metabolize it (without denying, running from, retaliating against, or attempting to rid ourselves of it).

S. Try to engage genius. (Don't focus on your child staying out of trouble.)

T. Strive for integrity. (Don't try to be good—read the essays: "Education" and "Character, Integrity, and Virtue.")

U. Find the right words. (Don't just repeat or say the wrong ones louder.)

V. If you don't like what's happening, change the game.

W. Let them teach you.

X. Remember: The child knows.

Y. Stop every fifty minutes and admire your work.

Z. Practice courage, persistence, authenticity, integrity, humility, forgiveness, charity, compassion, patience, mindfulness, trust, and humor.

# Acknowledgments

The creative work of an individual is almost always the result of community, communication, and conflict. This book is a good example. The ideas in it have been forged in dialogue, as great (and unfamous) people have come together over the years to work for children: conversations in an empty classroom, chats on the yard watching kids, discussions in meetings, talk around the table in the faculty lounge, and debates across my desk.

Most of the participants in the creation of this book have, therefore, been members of my school communities. Dialogue with teachers and parents about raising children and making school work for children have, over the years, produced a greater understanding among all of us about the dynamics of preparing children to be successful in the world today.

So, before I launch into trying to remember all the individuals who have contributed to this book, I need to thank all of my colleagues, students, parents of students and friends at the school communities of Notre Dame de Sion in Kansas City, The Cathedral School of St. John the Divine in New York City, St. Paul's Episcopal School in Oakland, California, and my current place of employment, Children's Day School in San Francisco. The dialogue continues to take us ever deeper into the challenges of raising children for an increasingly complex and changing world.

Many great teachers have been part of the reality-testing process over the years: Anola Picket, Peter Doyle, Ellen Baru, Joan Fitzpatrick, Fern Stampleman, Kit Land, Suzanne Abbey, Cinda Joyce, Judy Stone, Lee Davis, Matt Ronfelt, Susan Porter, Barbara De Moss, and Rebecca Kroll, to name a few. Many parents and friends have unknowingly effected important changes in my thinking, people like Peter and Sheila Dierks, Bob Conway, and Mark Lauden Crosley. Harvey Schwartz deserves special thanks for reading the entire manuscript in its early stages of formation and propelling the book forward with deep insights.

Among the many friends and colleagues at Children's Day School in San Francisco whose conversation, inspiration, and stories contributed to this book, two deserve special thanks: Bob Curly, former professor at the School of Education at the University of San Francisco, and Tracy Kirkham, six-year chair of the Board of Trustees. A number of the essays first appeared in some guise in my column in *The Children's Day School Weekly*. Therefore, Mary Denardo, Amanda Coggin, Julianna Bright, Marion Quinones, and Aimee Giles, deserve considerable credit and gratitude for improving on my rough drafts and steering my writing in good directions. Elizabeth McClellan, Gretchen Ott, Candy Mabry, Alicia Sheridan, and Margaret Piskitel contributed stories. Members of the school community who have read various drafts of the book and given me useful feedback are: John Hendrickson, Scott Brubaker, Winifred Von Ehrenberg, Louis Schump, Gary Strang, Jonathan Burton, Paul Minus, and Elsa Townsend.

I am blessed with a consistently supportive family. My brothers, Tod and Jim, have taken the time to read my writing over the years and given me helpful suggestions and encouragement. My adult offspring: Brooke, Peter, Lizzie, and Katie, conscientiously read my material and consistently gave me honest and useful feedback. They also gave me plenty to write about. I am grateful, too, that they have allowed me to go public with my stories about them. They continue to be an important part of my education. Special mention needs to be made that Brooke read two drafts of the manuscript in two successive summers and took the time to wrestle with me about everything from concept to organization. Her husband, Bill Zinke, not only put up with all this during one summer vacation, but also made useful contributions: the voice from the kitchen.

Sally Mahe, my ex-wife, whom I met at the Harvard Graduate School of Education in 1973, was not only my partner in raising all four of my children, but also a fellow educator. Twenty-two years of conversation with her have been a major contributor to my education and to this book indirectly.

Special acknowledgement goes to my sister Molly, who read every word of my original set of essays. She and my son Peter helped me focus on the challenge of resurrecting the original meaning of word "genius" and gave helpful advice about how that could be done successfully.

Many, many thanks to my official editors: Jennifer Manion at Beaver's Pond Press, and Miles McDonald who became my partner in the process. Laura Stevens from DivineCaroline.com, Dara Beevas from Beaver's Pond Press, and Rebecca Lawton, author and editor in Petaluma, California, have been very helpful and easy to work with. Kristen Hall is responsible for the lovely layout and Pat Rose of PR Communications has brought the book finally into print. I am especially grateful to John Hendrickson for championing the project and encouraging me to tell my story far and wide.

# ACKNOWLEDGMENTS

Most of all, I want to thank my wife, Victoria Podesta, whose commitment to telling the truth has resulted in her ability to be extremely skillful at it. Her criticism is always professionally and lovingly delivered, and her words are an important driver of my continuing intellectual development. I cling to the hope that her brilliance as a writer will somehow rub off a little on me.

In my practice of trying to help people change their behavior to get more of what they really want out of life, I have come to value the importance of good lines. Although my father, Dana C. Ackerly, was a brilliant inventor of memorable aphorisms, Victoria is the master. If in this book you find some good one-liners that help you with your children, credit my two mentors in the one-liner department: my father and my wife.

# Notes

1. *The Soul's Code: In Search of Character and Calling*, by James Hillman, Grand Central Publishing, 1997.

2. *Care of the Soul*, by Thomas Moore, HarperCollins, 1992.

3. *Mindset: The New Psychology of Success*, by Carol Dweck, Random House, 2006.

4. *Raising Lifelong Learners*, by Lucy Calkins, Da Capo Press, 1997.

5. "A Nation of Wimps," by Hara Estroff Marano, *Psychology Today*, Nov/Dec, 2004.

6. *The Hurried Child: Growing Up Too Fast Too Soon*, by David Elkind, Da Capo Press, 2001.

7. *Worried All the Time: Overparenting in an Age of Anxiety and How to Stop It*, by David Anderegg, Simon & Schuster, 2003.

8. *Putting Family First: Successful Strategies for Reclaiming Family Life in a Hurry-Up World*, by William J. Doherty and Barbara Z. Carlson, Macmillan, 2002.

9. *An Argument for Mind*, by Jerome Kagan, Yale University Press, 2007.

10. Solano Avenue Mental Health services. Sheri Glucoft-Wong, 1715 Solano Avenue, Berkeley, CA.

11. *Best Friends, Worst Enemies: Understanding the Social Lives of Children*, by Michael Thompson, Lawrence J. Cohen, and Catherine O'Neill Grace, Random House, 2002.

12. *Raising Lifelong Learners: A Parent's Guide,* by Lucy Calkins, Da Capo Press, 1997.

13. Research on the relationship between test scores and measures of adult effectiveness is covered thoroughly by Douglas Heath in *Maturity and Competence,* Gardner Press, 1977; again in *Fulfilling Lives,* Jossey-Bass, Inc., 1992; and summarized once more very effectively in his later book *Schools of Hope,* Jossey-Bass, 1994.

14. *The Disciplined Mind,* by Howard Gardner, Simon & Schuster, 2000.

15. *The Soul's Code,* by James Hillman, Grand Central Publishing, 1997.

16. *The Having of Wonderful Ideas,* by Eleanor Duckworth, Teachers College Press, 2006.

17. *Raising Lifelong Learners,* by Lucy Calkins, Da Capo Press, 1997.

18. "The Secret to Raising Smart Kids," by Carol S. Dweck, *Scientific American,* Nov. 28, 2007.

19. *Your Child's Strengths,* by Jenifer Fox, Viking Penguin, 2008.

20. *Handbook of Competence and Motivation,* Andrew J. Elliott and Carol Dweck, editors, The Gilford Press, 2005.

21. The relationship between praise, self-esteem, competence, self-confidence, ability, intelligence, and success has been thoroughly studied. *Handbook of Competence and Motivation* (see previous note) is a good place to start if one wanted to delve deeper. The term "self-esteem" has been used so much and now has so many definitions that studies of the relationship between "self-esteem" and success can show just about anything. I use the term "self-confidence" because it has a tighter meaning and does seem to correlate with success. Self-confidence is a little oblivious as to "positive and negative." A person's self-confidence is built on the experience of striving toward a goal which is related to one's needs, values, interests, and abilities, not on praise or even successful achievement of that goal. Praise does not hurt, and praising will keep happening with no harm done, because it is a way of saying, "I love you," but praise does not build competence and confidence.

22. *Extraordinary Minds*, by Howard Gardner, Perseus Book Group, 1998.

23. *The Importance of Mistakes*. A series including three videos: *Creativity in Management, The Hidden Mind*, and *The Importance of Mistakes*, all by John Cleese, John Cleese Business Training Videos, 2008.

24. *Five Minds for the Future*, by Howard Gardner, Libri, 2007.

25. *An Anthropologist on Mars*, by Oliver Sacks, Knopf, 1995.

26. Ibid.

27. *The Emotional Brain: The Mysterious Underpinnings of Emotional Life*, by J. LeDoux, Touchstone, 1996.

Also, for a useful summary of how emotions affect learning, a comprehensive article with a great set of references is "Emotions and Learning: Where Brain Based Research and Cognitive-Behavioral Counseling Strategies Meet the Road," by Carol A. Langelier and J. Diane Connell, *Rivier College Online Academic Journal*, Vol. 1, No. 1, Fall 2005.

28. *Ralph Waldo Emerson: Essays and Lectures*, The Library of America, 1992.

29. *Maturity and Competence*, by Douglas Heath, Gardner Press, 1977.

30. *A Farewell to Arms*, by Ernest Hemingway, Scribner's, 1929.

31. From *South Pacific*, a musical comedy by Richard Rodgers and Oscar Hammerstein II, 1949.

32. *The Little Prince*, by Antoine de Saint-Exupéry, Harcourt, 2000.

33. *A Mind That's Mine*, by Mel Levine, Simon & Schuster, 2002.

34. *The Person and the Situation: Perspectives of Social Psychology*, by Lee Ross, McGraw-Hill, 1991.

35. *Emotional Intelligence*, by Daniel Goleman, Bantam, 2005.

Made in the USA
Lexington, KY
25 May 2010